Legal and Ethical Issues in the Media

Key Concerns in Media Studies

Series editor: Andrew Crisell

Within the context of today's global, digital environment, *Key Concerns in Media Studies* addresses themes and concepts that are integral to the study of media. Concisely written by leading academics, the books consider the historical development of these themes and the theories that underpin them, and assess their overall significance, using up-to-date examples and case studies throughout. By giving a clear overview of each topic, the series provides an ideal starting point for all students of modern media.

Published

Andrew Crisell   *Liveness and Recording in the Media*

Tim Dwyer   *Legal and Ethical Issues in the Media*

Gerard Goggin   *New Technologies and the Media*

Shaun Moores   *Media, Place and Mobility*

Forthcoming

Paul Bowman   *Culture and the Media*

Bob Franklin   *Politics, News and the Media*

Gerard Goggin and Kathleen Ellis   *Disability and the Media*

David Hendy   *Public Service Broadcasting*

Niall Richardson and Sadie Wearing   *Gender and the Media*

Legal and Ethical Issues in the Media

Tim Dwyer

Senior Lecturer in Media and Communications,
University of Sydney, Australia

First published 2012 by
PALGRAVE MACMILLAN

Palgrave Macmillan in the UK is an imprint of Macmillan Publishers Limited, registered in England, company number 785998, of Houndmills, Basingstoke, Hampshire RG21 6XS.

Palgrave Macmillan in the US is a division of St Martin's Press LLC, 175 Fifth Avenue, New York, NY 10010.

Palgrave Macmillan is the global academic imprint of the above companies and has companies and representatives throughout the world.

Palgrave® and Macmillan® are registered trademarks in the United States, the United Kingdom, Europe and other countries.

ISBN-13: 978–0–230–24461–0

This book is printed on paper suitable for recycling and made from fully managed and sustained forest sources. Logging, pulping and manufacturing processes are expected to conform to the environmental regulations of the country of origin.

A catalogue record for this book is available from the British Library.

A catalog record for this book is available from the Library of Congress.

10   9   8   7   6   5   4   3   2   1
21   20   19   18   17   16   15   14   13   12

Printed and bound in Great Britain by
CPI Antony Rowe, Chippenham and Eastbourne

Contents

Acknowledgements

My sincere thanks go to Andrew Crisell, my Series Editor, for his many excellent suggestions for the book, and for his invitation to be involved in the series. My thanks also go to Tina Graham at Palgrave, and to Belinda Latchford.

I am grateful to colleagues in the Department of Media and Communications at the University of Sydney, for all the indirect assistance enabling me to undertake this writing project.

I am particularly grateful to Steven Maras and Anne Dunn for their exemplary foundational work in setting up the media law and ethics units of study in the Department. They did much of the pioneering hard work to establish these important programmatic areas of Sydney's media and communications degrees. Steven and I have co-taught the undergraduate media and law and ethics degree from 2008. I am indebted to him for his collegiality in sharing teaching materials and his conceptualization of these, particularly in relation to media ethics. He has influenced my thinking around many of these issues. My colleagues Gerard Goggin (and fellow series contributor) and Fiona Martin assisted through their responses to various corridor soundings and discussions.

I am indebted to the many enthusiastic local and international students as well as students from the diverse media and legal systems who have undertaken the postgraduate unit *Legal and Ethical Issues in Media Practice*; and who provided the ideal beta-test audience for much of the content of this book. Their shared media experiences and insights have greatly enriched the diversity of the unit, and informed my discussions of media, legal and ethical systems in the book.

A number of friends, colleagues and family made helpful editorial comments on draft versions of the manuscript. My thanks go to Michelle McAuslan and Steven Maras for their generous ideas for fine-tuning draft chapters; others have made useful teaching contributions, including Michael Mullins, Catherine Naylor, Jack Herman, Julian Morrow and Charles Firth. Colleagues in China and Japan were helpful interlocutors while I was researching and writing the book, including

Cao Jin (Fudan University), Stephen Quinn (*South China Morning Post*) and Shin Mizokoshi (University of Tokyo, Medialab). My brother, Greg Dwyer (Centre for Best Practice, College of Law, Sydney) made comments on draft chapters. My thanks also to A. J. and Graham Carter for sharing the Culburra weekender.

I thank the Faculty of Arts and Social Sciences, and in particular Annamarie Jagose, for supporting my research and writing, and approving the study leave that made the book possible.

Finally, I am indebted to Susan and Declan for all their suggestions and support.

1 Introduction

The role of media professionals working in the cultural and media industries is inevitably concerned with technical change, and transition in the practices of media production. But the enduring purposes of media to inform, educate and entertain remain a constant, in whichever order these are prioritized: an ethical media that informs a democratic citizenry is paramount. Climate change is nowadays referred to as the most important moral issue that human society faces in the twenty-first century, but without an ethically responsible media, very few people would have any idea about the actual significance of these developments.

The terms 'media', 'law' and 'ethics' get combined in various contexts. For some media students the first thought that comes to mind will be *Wire in the Blood* (2002–), *The Sopranos* (1999–2007), *Breaking Bad* (2008–), *Underbelly* (2008) or some other mediatized formats of criminality and general grievous bodily harm. For others it would be the illegal phone-hacking practices of tabloid media in their unauthorized intrusions into the lives of celebrities, politicians and even victims and their families. And for other people it might perhaps be the endlessly unethical practices of 'reality'-TV formats, and the way they treat their limelight-seeking contestants. The list of potential transgressive media practices is almost limitless, and even more so when we factor in new social media practices and internet cultures.

Yet knowing about these wider processes of mediatization assists us in gaining an understanding of the role of media in society, and has important implications for audiences' use of media, and the sense they make of the world. Our lives and our work increasingly involve engaging with large and small screens, some in our homes and others while we are on the move. We are informed, and entertained by and through media, and their access devices and applications are constantly evolving. This usage of mediatized content occurs in both public and private contexts, and this has divergent legal and ethical consequences and meanings for individuals, publics, cultures and societies.

This book is about examining the legal and ethical boundaries of media practices. Media practitioners learning the ropes need to develop an understanding of a range of key concepts, frameworks and general legal literacies that are relevant to their roles as content creators. On one level this is simply a matter of self-protection, but on another it is about acquiring the confidence to create well-informed, quality content for a media citizenry.

It is often not widely recognized by people who are just beginning their careers in the media, but if you have created, used or distributed content in a myriad of electronic ways, then you would have been bound by the same legal principles as journalists and other media workers who write or produce content for metropolitan dailies, for radio or television or 24/7 online.

Although it may not be necessary to have a lawyer's often detailed knowledge of laws, media practitioners need to be able to do risk assessments of the stories they write, or the content they produce. They need to be able to recognize risky words and phrases, know when to seek legal advice in relation to controversial content, estimate whether a publication is likely to land them in court and make informed judgments about whether to proceed with a publication.

The book also focuses on the ethical dimensions to media industries and media work. In broad terms, this means being aware that the foundations upon which those working in the media will often be making judgments and decisions, are informed by particular philosophies and belief systems. These range from formal religious and spiritual belief systems, through to less formal, less explicit and less self-conscious ideological and political frameworks of interpretation that exist in our everyday lives. Responsibility is an important concept for workers in the media industries who give voice to or represent ideas to often very large audiences. But without an understanding of what this responsibility entails, how can individual and organizational conduct be guided? Media academics James Curran and Jean Seaton famously counterposed what they regarded as a dominant fault-line in the moral history of media industries in the title of their landmark book, *Power without Responsibility: The Press, Broadcasting and New Media in Britain* (2003). Not surprisingly, this begs the questions: What is it to act responsibly in one's media practice, and for whose benefit? And how can those working in the media make sometimes difficult distinctions between their own agency, and the wider structural picture of the media industries?

In forming an understanding of divergent morality in media practices, it's important that we at least be aware of the main different
media systems. Ultimately, it's up to us as individuals to be in a position to use these comparisons to build our own memory databases of
different value assessments. Similarly, to achieve a global perspective
of difficult legal and ethical issues in the media we need to have a
sense of these different systems and their conditions. (We consider
different legal systems in Chapter 2.)

The rapidly changing media industries are driving new practices.
This is a dynamic process that is working in reverse too: new media
practices are influencing the way that the industry is evolving.
Facebook, Twitter, blogging and news forums, search engines and
video-sharing networks, are all being used in new ways that are
closely implicated in social change. The North African and Middle
Eastern democracy movements are just the latest examples in an
unfolding sequence of protest movements around the globe. Some
argue that all the while, running in the background, governments in
authoritarian states have twenty-four-hour media and communications machines that churn out alternative moral governance models
where 'economics trumps all' (French, 2011).

But the *moral* relationship of new social movements and the use of
new media practices is not just about revolutionary change. The ethical implications can be much more complex to tease out; they are
culturally and politically specific and arise from the particularities of
a national media-system context (Hallin and Mancini, 2004). My
approach in this book is to use examples from contemporary media
practice that assist us in unpacking legal and ethical nuance: no over-
arching ethical or legal model is privileged. My assumption is that
particular situations will have multiple determinations, affects and
meanings within a culture.

In China, as observed from around 2006, a rising phenomenon of
people power, mobilized through new media internet cultures, has
been reported. The notion of *human flesh search engines* translates into
Mandarin Chinese as *'renrou sousuo yinqing'*. One of the first widely
discussed instances of this phenomenon in the blogosphere involved
a short video that quickly spread virally on the internet. The video
depicted a stylishly dressed woman, standing on a riverbank, smiling,
with a small brown and white cat – which she then proceeds to
viciously kill under her silver stiletto shoe. Following this event, thousands of comments were posted on various online forums: 'This is not
a human'; 'Find her and kick her to death as she did to the kitten';

'Does anyone have a better image of this woman's face?' It was reported that before long the woman's personal details were freely available to netizens, and retribution came with the woman losing her job. Traditional media fuelled these discussions: for example, after the woman was identified, a China Central Television (CCTV) show called *News Investigation* conducted interviews (including one with the alleged perpetrator), and analyzed potential societal causes.

This process of mobilizing internet populations in China for vigilante-style 'payback' has been used to track down many individuals for a variety of perceived wrongs, from animal cruelty to corruption, to adultery. As Downey notes, 'It's crowd-sourced detective work, pursued online – with offline results' (ibid.). In these events the traditional media were very willing collaborators. Without their publicity, many events would not get the oxygen of wider public scrutiny. In the kitten killer's case, her photo became news on television and in newspapers all over China, and eventually the woman's identity and location were disclosed. It is a serious case involving new and old media, with complex ethical and legal dimensions.

So the human flesh search engines are fostering internet vigilantes, mobs, public shaming at best, and at worst, a kind of 'internet-lynching' mentality. People's personal details are sleuthed: their image, phone numbers, student ID, email and street address, work contacts, car licence-plate numbers. They can be tracked down when the power of collective intelligence is unleashed. On occasions the motives may be well intentioned, but on another level it is also 'public harassment, mass intimidation and populist revenge' (ibid.).

While a Chinese court has awarded very minor damages to an aggrieved individual because of the harm caused by an internet-service provider and a netizen, this is unlikely to have any significant longer-term impact on these *renrou sousuo yinqing* media practices. However, it's been suggested that new tort-law reform may encourage more of these lawsuits (ibid.).

How might we relate such practices to Western legal concepts? The doctrine of the *rule of law* may be invoked: it requires that several features will exist in common-law legal systems, or as American constitutional practice refers to it as, 'due process of law'. These include: independence of the judiciary; a speedy and fair trial; provision of adequate legal aid; the accused's right to refuse to make self-incriminating statements; advocacy free of state interference or pressures; the principle that a person is answerable for their own wrongdoing, and may not be subject to 'guilt by association' or group liability (Lloyd, 1981, pp. 162–5). Importantly, for media practitioners who report on such matters, the scope of the doctrine of the rule of law is not limited to safeguarding the rights of accused persons. It has an important dimension in the sphere of governmental and state powers more generally. This means that the rule of law, expressed as a principle of administrative law, has become embedded in the operation of courts or tribunals with supervision over executive levels of government or their agencies. This becomes very significant in situations of complaints against a government or a particular official.

The general absence of Western-styled rule of law and all that it entails, is fairly clear in these kinds of human-flesh-search-engines events, many would argue. Such an absence is, of course, largely expected in these dynamic new Chinese media cultures. The initial retributive conduct is virtual, but then it has very real-world, material, legal and ethical consequences. This can be seen in several examples of corrupt government officials being tracked down and ultimately exposed by netizens, and then this becomes amplified by traditional media. There is such an example in the report of an allegedly corrupt district official in Nanjing in charge of real estate, seen in an image posted on a website ostentatiously displaying his expensive Swiss watch. Despite the official's protests that the watch was a fake, he apparently lost his job. In another instance a Shenzhen local party official, seen drunk in a virally circulated video at a Communist Party event at a restaurant was caught on security camera verbally abusing the father of a young girl whom he had tried to molest in a washroom. This official also lost his job. There is the case of local jail administrators in rural Yunnan who were sacked after netizens were highly critical of their explanations for the head injuries of a prisoner. Initially, the jail administrators had claimed that the prisoner had been injured playing a 'blindman's bluff' game, but they were later forced to admit that he had been wilfully beaten to death. The former *Financial Times* China correspondent Richard McGregor suggests that the ruling Chinese Communist Party (CCP) had 'cannily leveraged a modern tool to keep sesame officials in line', which, in turn, allowed 'Chinese journalists and bloggers to expose local abuses of power in a way they never tolerate with senior officials in Beijing' (McGregor, 2010, p. 180). Rebecca McKinnon argues that this approach by Beijing is actually a rerun of an old Maoist idea of rising up against and reporting bourgeois or corrupt officials, a kind of 'Red Guard 2.0' (McKinnon in Downey, 2010).

For many, although 'justice' (broadly defined) might be the eventual outcome, clearly the legal and ethical elements of process were open to criticism. There is no assumption of innocence until proven guilty, no right to a fair trial or to privacy; these had been replaced by 'netizen rule'. Important tenets of Western liberal legal philosophy have been circumvented. But arguably there was majority or greater 'happiness' in John Stuart Mill's terminology, and perhaps the interest of the wider public was served? Moreover, if these are crowd-sourced investigations, with netizens sharing information and helping each other to publicly shame wrongdoers, isn't that for a good end? Is it not possible to argue that *renrou sousuo yinqing* practices are actually allowing contemporary Chinese citizens to work out, and healthily contest, moral priorities? While the West's obsession is more often than not about CCP control of media and censorship, the human-flesh-search-engines phenomenon is more accurately framed as being concerned with the everyday flow of information, and speech beyond the usual controls: and it can be a force for both good and less virtuous ideals, like anti-patriotism, anti-government protestors and racist vilification.

Not surprisingly, in the West we have some roughly similar phenomena, even if they're not identical. This point of overlap or intersection is very interesting, in an ethical sense, and draws our attention to more universalist values in different societies and their media cultures. Take this account of another woman, this time in the UK Midlands, rather than the Middle Kingdom, who is also not so enamoured of our feline companions. A forty-five-year-old Coventry woman, Mary Bale, was charged with a criminal offence of causing unnecessary suffering to a cat under the Animal Welfare Act 2006. Bale was caught on CCTV (closed circuit television) dumping a family cat into a large green wheelie bin as she walked past it. The cat was trapped for fifteen hours before being eventually freed by its owners. An online campaign led by the cat's owners to locate Bale ensued, with the video of the incident being posted to Facebook and YouTube (Parker, 2010). Before she was located and eventually arrested by police, she was named and shamed and the police arranged for community officers to stand watch outside her house to protect her against possible retribution (BBC, 2010). Bale was investigated by both the police and the RSPCA.

This incident has some common features with the human-flesh-search-engines cases in China. In both nations, vigilante action was mobilized via the internet and traditional media aided and abetted the process. While the Chinese netizens relied on popular web discussion forums for the circulation of information on individual wrong-doers, in the UK popular social-networking sites Facebook and YouTube were the preferred platforms. In both nations certain authorities are involved, although in China the role of the police is less clear. In all media cultures, the specific role of the media in representing these material practices has critical ethical implications for our societies. As a key concern over the transmission of media values, the question must be asked: How should news stories like the human flesh search engines be framed, and with what emphasis?

Framing Ethics for Media Practice

You might ask yourself what relevance does ethical philosophy have to a job in the media today? The answer is that media practitioners have a key role to play in the way moral debates actually work in society, are mediated, circulated and represented in the public sphere. In a market-driven and mediatized world, the priorities of information provision are defined by global infotainment conglomerates (Thussu, 2007; Spence *et al.*, 2011). Since transgressions of moral sensibilities occur incessantly in the media industries, more often than not under the guise of 'information that entertains', media workers are implicated in shaping the ethical landscape through their reports and opinions. As with the acquisition of legal concepts and knowledges, an understanding of important ethical-philosophy frameworks is also a matter of skilling up, educating and informing higher-quality media practices. For others, it will offer a toolkit for a better understanding of the ways that media work in our cultures and societies.

We will explore these frameworks again in more detail in Chapter 2 and throughout the book using selected media examples. However, for the purposes of an introductory discussion, we can consider some foundational concepts from ethical philosophy that assist us to unpack the ethical dilemmas confronting media practitioners. In addition to the 'three broad traditions of media ethicological discourse' (Crook, 2010, p. 156), namely, the deontological, the consequentialist and the virtuous, I include brief synopses of Christian, Foucauldian, Buddhist and Confucian ethics. These foundational concepts in ethical philosophy are not put forward here in any particular hierarchy or order of preference.

Virtue Ethics

Virtue ethics is sometimes also referred to as Aristotelianism or neo-Aristotelianism after its most well-known advocate from ancient Greece. An important original textual source of his philosophy was *The Nicomachean Ethics* (1999, 2004). This ethical philosophy emphasizes the whole character and the ability of individuals to 'improve' or 'flourish' over the course of their lives.

Aristotle's virtue theory is an example of moral rationalism, and focuses on the character of people in terms of their virtues. As a form of moral rationalism it can be encapsulated in the idea that it is more important to travel than to arrive. That is, we can improve our understanding of moral problems, both major ones like poverty, war, capital punishment, etc. (and all the broader value systems they imply) and relatively minor ones such as how we, for example, represent someone that we've interviewed or described in a media story. It is referencing a model of ethical conduct that considers that individuals are capable of, and indeed should strive and be responsible for, self-improvement in the way that they deal with ethical issues. Aristotelian ethics is sometimes referred to as a teleological ethics from the Greek *'telos'*, meaning 'ends'. Virtue theory is an ethics of ends; an account of how a person's character may reach a virtuous endpoint. A contemporary equivalent, which finds resonances in several of the ethical frameworks in this chapter, is the idea of 'displaying one's moral compass'. Individuals can learn to fine-tune their moral decision-making apparatuses and find *the good life*.

Some terminology is key to understanding Aristotle's virtue ethics. The term *eudaimonia* was the word Aristotle used in his virtue ethics to describe a person who had arrived at a state of 'well-being', flourishing in a mentally active way, and enjoying life (Graham, 2004, p. 54). The Greek word *'arete'* translates to 'virtue', so in *The Nicomachean Ethics*, the phrase 'in accordance with virtue' means that we should approach any particular set of moral circumstances 'in the best possible way'. Aristotelian virtue ethics employs the term *'phronesis'* or 'practical wisdom' to emphasize that sheer intellectual insight alone is not the path to the good life. Rather, it's a combination of intellect and emotional intelligence that has been cultivated through life choices that would represent 'the good' for humans (ibid., p. 57).

This emphasis on making the right decision to fit a particular set of circumstances is informed by the notion of a *golden mean* (Graham, 2004). But this was not a matter of simply steering to the middle ground in making the best possible ethical decision: it is a reference to a notion of balancing between the extremes that may arise in certain contexts. Crook's view is that this is concerned with 'good motives, and determining good actions to achieve good consequences' (2010, p. 157). Virtue ethics, then, requires a deft balancing act between extremes of emotions and rationality. There is a view that virtue ethics is well suited for application as an ethical framework in media-practice contexts since it recognizes the role of individual moral agency, above black-and-white laws, regulations or codes of practice; and that a virtuous character is very important when it comes to making decisions including those related to media production (Black and Roberts, 2011; Couldry, 2006). The notion of a golden mean can be traced back to a century before Aristotle, in Confucian thought, and it offers a way to negotiate or 'moderate' between conflicting positions in 'practical situations in everyday media environments' (Bugeja, 2008, p. 26).

Nick Couldry, a leading British media scholar, is a 'neo-Aristotelian', and he applies his contemporary virtue ethics to theorize the performance of the media, *and* how people make use of the media around them. One of his key arguments is that the media play a vitally important role in the circulation of information helpful to the conduct of citizens' lives (Couldry, 2006, p. 125). However, human agency remains the starting point for his media ethics, and this means that, in order to act responsibly, we need to think carefully about how we use available media, but also that media practitioners should strive to lead more ethical professional lives.

Deontological Ethics

The term 'deontological ethics' is from the Greek '*deon*' meaning duty. The most prominent figure in this tradition of ethical philosophy is Immanuel Kant, who was born in 1724 in Konigsberg, Prussia, and died in 1804. Central to Kantian ethical precepts is the idea that actions should be judged according to the intentions that motivate them. Individuals' own sense of self-directed internal moral duty is determinative, not whether the consequences will retrospectively justify a certain course of action.

Many of the central aspects of Kant's ethics derive from his *Fundamental Principles of the Metaphysics of Morals* (1785) and his *The Critique of Practical Reason* (1787). Kant developed an elaborate scheme of categorical imperatives based on specific maxims such as

'Act only according to the maxim which you can at the same time will that it should become a universal law.' Actions are judged right in this framework if they follow a certain moral rule that satisfies a categorical imperative. The Christian overtones in Kant's ethics are inescapable, for example in the maxim 'Act so that you treat humanity, whether in your own person or in that of another always as an end, and never as a means only' (McCormack, 2006 cited in Crook, 2010, p. 181). The latter maxim is usually referred to as the *humanity principle*. In media work, it brilliantly gives pause to ethical decision-making and guides moral actions. However, it also creates potentially insurmountable ethical dilemmas for media-practice routines, since on some level individuals are interviewed or incorporated in narratives in the making of media products, and are therefore *always* a means to an end. This is not, of course, to foreclose the myriad ways in which ethical thinking can be brought to bear on situations confronting media practitioners on a daily basis.

Kant's ethics then, is very rule-based, and therefore resonates with a more legalistic or 'black letter' law or codes-based approach to problem solving, including those arising from media practice. His focus was on obligation, fulfilling our duties and leading our everyday lives in a responsible manner (Black and Roberts, 2011, p. 340). Gordon Graham has suggested that Kantian ethics is 'marred' in at least two ways. First, since will or intention is privileged and bracketed from consequences, this sets up 'a complete divorce', which is impossible. Second, he argues that, although we can agree that will or intention must be an important component in weighing up moral actions, the prerequisite for universal application of reasons for acting in particular ways is a flawed test. If any set of actions or mode of conduct can be universally described as the best moral outcome, it cannot hope to account for nuance or exceptional situations (Graham, 2004, p. 122).

In spite of these criticisms of deontological ethics and its most famous advocate, as an approach it represents an invaluable touchstone for ethical decision-making, especially to those who work in the media. The moral duties for people in the media industry are many: to be fair and honest, to be accurate, to protect individual privacy especially when gathering news information, to be cautious when media production involves children, to protect the anonymity of sources and so on. That a Kantian ethics is in many ways a theological pathway to explore, sets itself up to occupy a 'high moral ground'. For many, including media practitioners, that can be a safe, indeed superior, position to occupy.

Christian Ethics

With many connections to Kantian moral duty and more absolutist values, a Christian ethics can be construed as a populist framework relied on in decision-making in all spheres of activity, including the media. The idea of 'Do unto others as you would have them do unto you' is quite close to the (Kantian) humanity principle's prescribed conduct towards others. Although a predominantly secular understanding of the interaction of law and morality is mainstream thinking now, except in relation to particular religious traditions, that has not always been the case (Lloyd, 1981, p. 46). In earlier historical periods it was normal for morality, law and religion to interact. Of course this connection of laws to divinity is embedded in the popular imagination through our knowledge of the Ten Commandments (or 'the Decalogue').

Conduct is strongly circumscribed by an either/or view of whether or not it conforms to the Christian moral code. As an infallible guide to the correct behaviour in any context, a Christian ethics is said to be the following of God's will. Conduct tends to be reduced to a calculus of whether it is right or wrong under this Christian code, in all its multifarious variants. It may surprise some to contemplate the idea that, in some fundamental ways, Christian ethical frameworks are similar to those of other monotheistic religions such as Islam and Judaism. These religions all share a view that the correct way to live is to observe codes prescribed in the writings of a supreme deity, which make up a master rule-book for a moral life.

A Christian ethics shares with several of the frameworks discussed the notion that it is possible to develop morally by making judgment calls over a life. This can be defined as character building for a better life, acting on a sense of duty and conscience, following the right path in one's professional or personal life or selecting the elements that appear to be true or consistent with your beliefs and approach to living with others. In our media practice, it makes sense that we are guided by our wider beliefs and values: these form an underlying scaffolding for those who chose not to draw distinctions between their personal or working lives; or for that matter, the particular media platform they are making media texts on, as we are now all exposed to cross-media work (Bugeja, 2008, p. 3).

Utilitarian Ethics

Utilitarianism, which is also referred to as a consequentialist approach, is interested in the consequences of actions and decisions, rather than the intentions behind them, or the moral duty or character of the person responsible for them.

Utilitarianism can take many different forms. It is popularly associated with Jeremy Bentham (1748–1832) and John Stuart Mill (1806–73). In English literature, utilitarianism is immortalized in Dickensian notions of an approach interested solely in usefulness rather than beauty or pleasantness (Graham, 2004, p. 129). The 'workhouses' of Victorian England were 'useful' in the sense that they provided a roof over the heads of people otherwise forced through poverty to live on the streets, but happiness was a rare commodity.

However, it was not usefulness in the modern sense of 'utility' that interested utilitarian ethical philosophers. So, how might we best characterise a utilitarian ethics? Its fundamental premise is that decisions should be made according to the amount of happiness particular actions or conduct will promote. The *greatest happiness principle* is closely associated with utilitarianism, and advocates actions that are likely to lead to the maximum amount of 'happiness' or pleasure in any given situation. Mill expressed it this way: 'actions are right in proportion as they tend to promote happiness, and wrong as they tend to produce the reverse of happiness' (Mill, 1976, p. 117)

The main difficulty from a media-practice perspective is that utilitarianism as an ethical framework may provide a justification for many actions in popular entertainments, including media treatments of various issues and concerns that satisfy the majority of people. In other words, an action is deemed 'ethical' if it results in a large number of happy people; rather than whether or not it improved or corrected some social situation, or the welfare of certain individuals or disadvantaged groups. As you might anticipate, this formula for media practice privileges maximum pleasure and entertainment, and is also likely to be a high-ratings winner, even if it causes harm to certain people in the process. The other important implication pointed out by Graham, is that utilitarianism is not an altruistic ethical or moral philosophy: although promoting a generalized happiness, it's more concerned with individual happiness and in this sense might be considered to be an attitude of 'generalized benevolence' (Graham, 2004, p. 134).

The distinction between so-called act- and rule-utilitarianism is an important feature of this ethical framework. This might be best explained through an example from contemporary cinema. In the film *28 Days Later* (2002) directed by Danny Boyle, humanity is on the verge of annihilation due to the rapid spread of a plague-like virus known as 'rage'. Those infected suffer a slow and crazed death, and attack the unafflicted, thus spreading the virus. In the film, it is acceptable for survivors to kill other humans in order to preserve their own lives. This might be interpreted from within the bounds of an act- and rule-utilitarian ethical framework. In this 'end-of-humanity' scenario, the taking of human life is condoned, and implied to be morally justified. Act-utilitarianism would decree that, generally speaking, the happiness and greatest pleasure of the majority requires that humans do not kill each other under any circumstances. However, a rule-utilitarian ethical framework would allow that, in these horrific conditions, it is permissible to take a life, or multiple lives, to ensure healthy individuals' survival *and* the survival of the species. In other words, while the act-utilitarian would suggest every action is taken in order to maximize happiness, the rule-utilitarian would say that, if our actions follow the rules, then the greatest happiness will ensue. The general prohibition against killing is there for good reason and allows the majority to live together peacefully, most of the time. This is the utilitarian ethical framework, but as amended by Mill, who saw exceptions to the general 'act-utilitarianism' approach, that would, on occasion, require rules for the greatest happiness and even justice (ibid., p. 136).

Cees Hamelink has argued in *The Ethics of Cyberspace* that both act-utilitarianism and rule-utilitarianism are ultimately flawed for two reasons. First, who decides who is the supreme agent defining the optimal consequences for certain choices; and second, how can we gauge those ideal consequences in disparate situations (and in rule-utilitarianism situations sufficiently similar for a rule) for different actors? In other words, the consequences (actual effects) for the largest number of people are not always foreseeable (Hamelink, 2000, pp. 3–4). Nonetheless, this ethical approach is capable of provoking serious debate about moral choices (especially in media-production decisions) and their consequences.

Other specific media examples throughout the book will invoke utilitarian thinking, but you will gain a sense of how this framework may be used to justify practices such as invasion of privacy through surreptitious filming, the use of listening devices and forms of entrapment and deceit. Some media codes of practice contain clauses which consider the consequences of actions for an individual's privacy, when they are subject to covert surveillance, and generally when information is being gathered about them. In those circumstances, media workers would need to fully assess the broader 'public-interest' merits of these kinds of secretive activities (see Chapters 4 and 5).

We can see that weighing up consequences and calculating the amounts of happiness or pleasure generated by a particular media story, programme, blog, website or tweet is a helpful framework for media practitioners. The contentious aspects of this framework, however, are connected with whether the evaluative process is reliable, and whether or not there are other preferable frameworks to assist decision-making and judgment in media practice.

Foucauldian Ethics

The philosophy of Michel Foucault can make an important contribution to our understanding of media ethics. As one of the major ethical philosophers of the modern period, Foucault's thought can be usefully applied to the steady stream of controversy and scandals in the media. Indeed media scholars are seeing the explanatory value of Foucault's work from a number of different perspectives. For example, Albury, in her research on pornography, argues that the ways in which individuals negotiate an understanding of their own ethical position through 'a personal and community-based process', align well with the philosopher's writings in relation to how people reflect on and construct their personal ethical sensibilities (Albury, 2003, pp. 206–7). McCluskie, on the other hand, suggests Foucault's contribution lies in making available a powerful critique that allows us to see how relations between 'knowledge regimes' and 'concrete practices' shape individual actions. Further, McCluskie argues that 'panoptic control' and the industrial ramifications of, for instance, 'the declining/reconfigured ranks of reporters' are relevant to a contemporary media ethics (McCluskie, 2011, p. 371). For industries that are constantly evolving, Foucault's legacy for media ethics is both in providing tools to assist us in analyzing industrial operations on the big-picture canvas of changing practices; and, at the same time, in examining at a very personal level the way that individuals make their own sense, and find their way ethically, within the media industries.

In 1984 Foucault died, aged 57, leaving a huge legacy in terms of his contribution to philosophy and the number of influential texts he authored. The actual corpus is very well known, including key works such as *Madness and Civilisation* (1961); *The Order of Things* (1966); *The Archaeology of Knowledge* (1972); *The Birth of the Clinic* (1973); *Discipline and Punish* (1975) and *The History of Sexuality* (1976, 1984, 1984) (Rabinow, 2000).

The ancient Greeks in the sixth and seventh centuries BC provided considerable historical source materials for Foucault, particularly in the truthful discourses of the poets. In an inaugural lecture at the College de France, 'The Order of Discourse', Foucault outlined the goals of his philosophical project, in broad terms, as questioning human beings' *will to truth*, to 'restore to discourse its character as an event and in short to 'abolish the sovereignty of the signifier' (Rabinow, 2000, p. XII). His work is also based on related ideas of a 'will to knowledge', 'systems of exclusion', 'technologies of power' and 'technologies of the self'.

In 'On the Genealogy of Ethics', Foucault seeks to elaborate on an ethics, or personal conduct, as an 'aesthetics of existence' (Foucault, in ibid., p. 261). Following from his analysis of wider personal relations, including sexual relations among the ancient Greeks, Foucault argues that humans should see their own everyday lives as a kind of work of art. It's a view that people can exercise a certain aesthetic activism and agency over how they constitute themselves, through the personal choices they make. There are, then, visible elements of the other ethical philosophies: Aristotelian virtue ethics, Christian ethics and Confucian ethics. As in virtue ethics, we can see that individuals can make conscious decisions about how they build their own moral self. It's a kind of self-directed ethics where different components can be selected and assembled in ways that we as individuals believe best represent ourselves as moral agents.

In his major three-volume treatise, *The History of Sexuality*, Foucault was analyzing the history of morals. He was able to distinguish certain acts or actions on the one hand, and moral codes that may apply to them on the other. He uses the example of relations between a man and a woman, governed by a marital code, which sets down certain rules about only being allowed to have sex within the marriage, not with others. Overlying these prescriptions on our moral lives is something Foucault refers to as *rapport à soi*, which translates as 'the relationship with one's self'. By this he means that, in addition to the moral requirements and prescriptions that apply socially, and institutionally, there's also this process of moral self-manufacturing.

Foucault believed that this relationship with one's self could be broken down into several different sub-elements. First, there is the aspect concerned with moral conduct, whether we refer to that in a Christian sense as feelings, a Kantian sense as intention, or a Foucauldian sense as our response to a particular judgment or ethical decision. In a media-practice context this ethical substance might refer to the choices we have made in constructing a story or some media product. Myriad choices and decisions are made in our media practice: what is omitted is frequently as significant as what is included. An important dimension, then, of Foucault's ethics is the cumulative affects of our ethical decision-making, as constitutive of our wider moral lives over time. In this sense it is like an Aristotelian virtue ethics, which similarly advocates moral development.

Second, Foucault saw that the relationship to one's self contained a 'mode of subjectivation' or *mode d'assujettissement*, which refers to the way people are interpolated or called into recognizing their moral position or obligations. Here Foucault is referring to whether the source of a particular moral ideology is, for example, a 'natural law' (against murdering fellow humans), a universal rule in a Kantian sense (some general prohibition) or more to do with an aesthetics of existence (a conscious personal decision that is consistent with one's own moral agency).

Third, how can we as individual subjects mould our own morality in order to become ethical actors? Foucault believed this was about what individuals can do for themselves, in their own self-formation or asceticism.

Fourth, Foucault considered that the relationship with ourselves was about the *telos*, or becoming. This could be framed as 'best practice' for the self: what kind of being do we aspire to the most? So overall, there are moral codes of behaviour or conduct (and this is not referring to the media codes of practice, principles or standards), which exist in society and its institutions, and then there are the processes over which we can direct or participate in our own self-construction, in a moral sense. His argument is that together these two elements constitute the sphere we call 'morals' (ibid., pp. 263–4).

Foucauldian ethics covers a great deal of terrain as a history of morality and examine the role that 'technologies of the self' play in moral processes. He is imputing more to a subject's constitution than mere immersion in a 'symbolic system' (ibid., p. 277). Individuals are assembling their own moral agency from a range of available resources; a process that requires living and character formation in an Aristotelian sense. Foucault's ethical philosophy is sometimes criticized as being too morally relativistic or ambiguous. However, to be broadly comparative is often a good way to make moral judgments across society and cultures. On the other hand, if values are intentionally contrarian or anti-universalistic, that may also be very problematic in the group decision-making processes that often occur in media contexts.

For media practitioners, the power of Foucault's ethical reasoning perhaps derives from his recognition of moral diversity itself. This is an appealing proposition for those who value media diversity.

Foucauldian ethics represent an important contribution to interpretative, contextually generated, inductive moral decision-making in media practice.

Confucian Ethics

Aristotelian virtue ethics finds considerable resonance in the ethics of Confucius. As with Aristotle's ethics, Confucian ethics has as its starting point a reflection on human life overall, rather than specific acts or conduct, and focuses on human character rather than rules, principles or consequences. For both Aristotle and Confucius the concern is with what a 'good life' is, or how a person can lead a good life, and what qualities are necessary to do so.

There are some fundamental steps for taking a Confucian approach to ethics. Rather than a focus on Aristotle's *eudaimonia* (happiness, thriving) Confucius (551–479 BCE) sought to find the human *dao* (way), or the path to become a good person. To become a good person, one must cultivate *de*, that is, a dispositional character (generally translated as 'virtue' in English) or the character *ren*. *Ren* has been generally translated as 'benevolence' or 'humanity', but is also widely referred to as 'human virtue' or 'cardinal virtue' (Yu, 2007, p. 24). Just as *eudaimonia* or 'happiness' is the pursuit of virtue ethics, *dao*, or the way, is the common object of ancient Chinese ethics. Confucian ethics is called '*dao* of the Master', so in that sense Confucian teachings are also a discourse about an ethical method.

In Chinese intellectual history the ideas of Confucius often stem from the 'Four Books', including the *Analects, Mencius, The Great Learning (Daixue)* and the *Doctrine of the Mean (Zhongyong)*. In elaborating how it is that a person can become a good person by cultivating *ren*, Confucian ethics reflects on and discusses all the core living issues including what it is to be human and lead a good life, education, family, virtue politics and so on.

In a Confucian ethics, a key question is 'Where is the human *dao*?' Thus, in seeking out the best ethical approach to a particular issue, people need to reflect on their lives and ask if they are on the correct path for a 'good life'? (ibid., p. 27). This is obviously a question that many media practitioners could certainly benefit from asking themselves, in the context of thinking through the implications and consequences of the media content they produce. We only need to observe the excesses of commercial radio or the havoc wrought in the lives of 'reality'-television-show contestants to understand the importance of such reflection. Confucius saw his role as a 'transmitter' of traditional values and ideals. The underlying purpose of this transmission was the perpetuation of the *dao* embodied in these traditional values (ibid., p. 45). The parallels for media practitioners are unavoidable, even if 'missionary' pursuit of virtuous objectives is not a prime motivation.

Buddhist Ethics

A relatively new, and yet vast field that has rarely been applied specifically to media practice, especially outside the Asian region, Buddhist ethics is seen to have a close relation to Buddhist philosophy itself. Indeed the notion that a moral life and decision-making are intimately connected with the typical mental cultivation associated with Buddhist ethics makes a persuasive argument (Hallisey, 2003).

If notions of 'cultivation', 'perfection', 'habituation' and 'improvement' sound similar to the Aristotelian virtue ethics' ideal of character formation and becoming an ethical person, that is not surprising. Writers of Buddhist ethics acknowledge the connection, and agree that 'virtue' is a common dimension shared with the ancient Greek ethicists. But it's worth remembering that Buddhism as a religious philosophy pre-dates the Greeks (Plato, Socrates) by several centuries. As Saddhatissa notes, writing in the Theravada Buddhist tradition, a learned and eminent Brahman 'expounded his teaching that morality and wisdom are essential to the character of a true Brahman', representing the ideal, ethical person (Saddhatissa, 2003). It is in this context of normative evaluations of the character of people that a Buddhist ethics is well positioned to offer decision-making guidance for media practitioners. However, Buddhist ethics is a very broad field of philosophical inquiry and 'mind culture' generally, and therefore has a great deal to offer thinking about relations to media representations and practices.

Structure of the Book

The purpose of this chapter was to introduce readers to the importance of media practitioners possessing a toolkit of legal, ethical and media-practice skills and knowledges, in order to produce quality content for an informed citizenry. The issues, concepts and ethical frameworks introduced in this chapter are a useful starting point for reflecting on ethical media practice. In Chapter 2 we continue to consider these literacies through an exploration of some of the basic constituent elements of interacting legal, ethical and media systems. Chapter 3 considers confidential information and defamation across Anglophone common-law jurisdictions and cultures, while in Chapter 4, evolving notions of privacy are explored through a discussion of the uses of new media and communications technologies.

Chapter 5 delves into the shifting debates in relation to intellectual property and modes of regulation. Copyright is examined in the context of the realignment of technological capacities and media-consumption practices, where the long-term sustainability of this business model, for both rights holders and consumers, is uncertain. Chapter 6 draws on a case study of large-scale corporate media consolidation to explore the contemporary application of the term 'public interest': the argument is made that key ethical questions arise from the fundamental structuring of media systems in market societies. In the concluding chapter we review enduring risks and priorities for media practitioners, who find themselves operating in the midst of ongoing transformations in the media and communications industries.

References

Albury, K. (2003) 'The Ethics of Porn on the Net', in C. Lumby and E. Probyn (eds) *Remote Control: New Media, New Ethics* (Cambridge: Cambridge University Press).

Aristotle (1999) *The Nicomachean Ethics*, 2nd edn, Terence Irwin (trans.) (Indianapolis, IA: Hackett Publishing, Inc).

Aristotle (2004) *The Nicomachean Ethics*, J. A. K. Thomson (trans.) (London: Penguin Books).

BBC (2010) 'Woman Filmed Dumping Cat in Wheelie Bin in Coventry', available online at http://www.bbc.co.uk/news/uk-england-coventry-warwickshire-11068063.

Black, J. and C. Roberts (2011) *Doing Ethics in Media: Theories and Practical Applications* (Milton Park and New York: Routledge).

Bugeja, M. (2008) *Living Ethics: Across Media Platforms* (New York: Oxford University Press).

Couldry, N. (2006) *Listening beyond the Echoes: Media, Ethics, and Agency in an Uncertain World* (Boulder, CO: Paradigm Publishers).

Crook, T. (2010) *Comparative Media Law and Ethics* (Milton Park and New York: Routledge).

Curran, J. and J. Seaton (2003) *Power without Responsibility: The Press, Broadcasting and New Media in Britain*, 6th edn (London: Arnold).

Downey, T. (2010) 'China's Cyberposse', *NYTimes.com*, available online at http://www.nytimes.com/2010/03/07/magazine/07Human-t.html?_r=1& hp=&pagewanted=all.

Foucault, M. (2000) 'On the Genealogy of Ethics: An Overview of Work in Progress' [excerpt], in *Michel Foucault, Ethics: Subjectivity and Truth*, Paul Rabinow (ed.) (London: Penguin Books), pp. 253–71.

French, H. W. (2011) 'The View of Cairo from Authoritarian International', *Atlantic.com*, 11 February.

Graham, G. (2004) *Eight Theories of Ethics* (London: Routledge).

Hallin, D. C. and P. Mancini (2004) *Comparing Media Systems: Three Models of Media and Politics* (Cambridge: Cambridge University Press).

Hallisey, C. (2003) 'Introduction', in H. Saddhatissa, *Buddhist Ethics* (Somerville, MA: Wisdom Publications).

Hamelink, C. (2000) *The Ethics of Cyberspace* (London, Thousand Oaks, CA and New Delhi: Sage).

Lloyd, D. (1981) *The Idea of Law* (Harmondsworth: Penguin Books).

McCluskie, E. (2011) 'Media Ethics as Panoptic Discourse: A Foucauldian View', in R. S. Fortner and P. Mark Fackler (eds) T*he Handbook of Global Communication and Media Ethics*, Vol. 1 (Malden, MA: Wiley).

McGregor, R. (2010) *The Party: The Secret World of China's Communist Rulers* (London and New York: Allen Lane/Penguin).

Mill, J. S. (1976) 'What Utilitarianism Is', in *John Stuart Mill on Politics and Society*, Geraint L. Williams (ed.) (New York: International Publication Service).

Parker, A. (2010) 'Cruel Woman Dumps Cat in Bin', *TheSun.co.uk*, available at http://www.thesun.co.uk/sol/homepage/news/3107733/Cruel-woman-dumps-cat-in-bin.html.

Rabinow, P. (ed.) (2000) *Michel Foucault. Ethics: Subjectivity and Truth* (London: Penguin Books).

Saddhatissa, H. (2003) *Buddhist Ethics* (Somerville, MA: Wisdom Publications).

Spence, E. H., A. Alexandra, A. Quinn and A. Dunn (2011) *Media, Markets, and Morals* (Malden, MA and Oxford: Wiley-Blackwell).

Thussu, D. (2007) *News as Entertainment: The Rise of Global Infotainment* (London, Thousand Oaks, CA, New Delhi and Singapore: Sage).

Yu, J. (2007) *The Ethics of Confucius and Aristotle: Mirrors of Virtue* (New York: Routledge).

2 Legal, Ethical and Media Systems

This chapter will consider the questions: What are some of the key elements of our legal, ethical and media systems, and how do they interact? Why should we study media law, ethics and media systems together? The inference made is that the wider context of considering the media with legal and ethical processes is a changing media system itself. This juxtapositioning of systems may at first seem forebodingly 'functionalist' and somehow out of step with postmodern social and cultural developments in our mediatized world. However, my argument is that, for comparative purposes, a 'systems' view is entirely appropriate. When I talk with students about the media and their legal or ethical frameworks 'back home', they are very likely to say that xyz issue can be explained in a particular way because their country has 'a different *system*'. This recognition of cultural and national differences must be at the heart of any serious attempt to comparatively analyze the way legal and ethical issues arise in particular nation-states. There will, of course, be points of intersection and commonality, but there will also be dramatic departures because of contextually divergent social, cultural and political traditions in different legal, ethical and media systems.

When we look across cultures and 'systems', we inevitably bump up against issues that have more universal elements, and this will become apparent in some of the examples we discuss. However, in this chapter we focus on some of the foundations that media students should know as part of their legal literacy in common-law legal systems. For example, this will include, importantly, the main sources of law in statutes and common law. It is not necessary to have a lawyer's knowledge but media practitioners do need to be aware of risky words or phrases, and to recognize situations where they should seek specialized legal advice. But my argument is that media practitioners need to learn some specific concepts and literacies: the doctrine of precedent, open justice, the right to a fair trial, freedom of speech and rules about reporting the courts, including contempt of court.

My purpose in this chapter is to foster an interdisciplinary perspective that will not be solely legal, nor just about ethical philosophical or critical media-studies analysis. This means that we can draw on ethical philosophy and legal studies, cultural studies, political science and political economy at different times, depending on the issue at hand. Morality interacts with our processes of judgment, deliberation and reasoning in the study of legal, ethical and media systems. At such sites we can use these multiple disciplinary perspectives, and practitioner perspectives – legal, ethical and media industry ones – to reflect on and assess particular moments of 'mediatization'. Thomas De Zengotita's view in his book *Mediatized* is that mediatization in a postmodern world is operating at the level of common sense and 'in that awareness, the ethos of mediation is established' (De Zengotita, 2005). My suggestion is that monitoring the media from legal and ethical perspectives involves analyzing the everyday construction of news and events by the media.

Laws, governance, ethics and media are behind many pressing issues in contemporary society and culture. As mediatized communications become ever more part of our everyday lives, they also become a part of our commonsense understanding of ways to live our lives. It's important also to situate our everyday engagements with diverse media forms and practices in relation to the forces that are restructuring the media industries. Equally, the ways in which people are using media are directly linked to complex, multilayered interactions between 'traditional' media and communication cultures and new online and mobile media.

Legal Systems around the Globe

Although I am writing this book situated within a Westminster-style, common-law system, teaching in a university with an internationalized student cohort provides a reality check that many students will have a rather different understanding of the meaning of the term 'legal system'. As national political systems themselves vary, so too will the legal systems from which they are derived and the media systems that report them.

Living in cosmopolitan societies, in a globally interconnected world, the key objective in being aware of these different legal systems is to become better informed, and thus less likely to sit in judgment of other systems, produced by their own unique historical and cultural circumstances. To do otherwise becomes ethnocentric and overly reliant on the perspective of one's own system as a normative benchmark.

In this chapter I will first give a brief account of these systems, and second, consider some vivid examples that serve as a way to compare at a glance some of the obvious departures between them. My intention is not to be reductive or to oversimplify, but rather to highlight some basic differences between these national legal contexts. This has important implications for how the media actually operate within those social, cultural and political contexts.

Jago and Fionda (2005, p. 5 in Crook, 2010) categorize the four major legal jurisdictions (or systems) of the world:

- common law
- civil law
- socialist law
- Islamic law.

Crook argues that, 'the researcher needs to freeze or discount stereotypical assumptions of how media law and ethics should work, and endeavour to investigate and understand the religious beliefs, history, constitution, social values and political system of a specific country'. He also notes: 'The relativist perspective focuses on an understanding of a media law system by examining the differences and relationships within the cultural and social contexts of the country under investigation' (2010, p. 355). He believes that researchers can avoid 'criminological tourism' and making ill-informed judgments on the basis of wearing metaphorical 'rose-tinted intellectual spectacles' that may lead to a superficial cultural misunderstanding.

The following section will consider some of the key elements of each legal system. Even based on this limited set of characteristic features, armed with this knowledge, students are less likely to make ethnocentric judgments. This may be in part relativistic and universalist from the perspective of ethical philosophy, but it seems to me that this is an advantage for those wishing to compare media-system events across cultures. The purpose of this brief review is to provide a sense of how these systemic features may then work to shape relations between citizens, and between citizens and the state.

Common Law

In broad terms the common-law legal system refers to the system where law is made by judges and is originally derived from the English legal system. Countries with common-law systems include Australia, the UK, the US, New Zealand, Canada, Hong Kong, Malaysia, Singapore, India, Ireland and South Africa, among others.

There are two main sources of law: statutes (made by the legislature/ politicians at the state or federal level) and judge-made common law or case law. Common law is based on an important principle known as the 'doctrine of precedent'. Courts are bound to follow the decisions of courts superior to them in the court hierarchy. This principle is sometimes also known as *stare decisis*. Decisions of other common-law jurisdictions may be 'persuasive' (or influenced by) but not 'binding' (bound to follow) unless they involve a superior court (e.g. in Australia, a State District Court is bound by a decision in the Supreme Court and the High Court). When judges determine that the facts in a particular case are sufficiently different or 'distinguished' from another one, they may make new law arising from the fact scenarios of the matter under consideration. The generally malleable character of common-law legal systems means that they are, in theory at least, well suited to responding to evolving social and cultural change, subject to the usual limits imposed in, for instance, liberal democracies, where the interests of powerful lobby and special-interest groups will tend to prevail.

Under the common-law system, where there is both legislation and a court decision on the same matter, the legislation will take priority. In this sense, common law can be differentiated from areas of law deriving from statutes, such as criminal law (sometimes 'codified'), procedural, contract law, tort law, constitutional law or other statutes governing forms of regulatory law, as is often the case for media and communications.

Civil Law

Civil law is the most widely adopted legal system in the world, and can be seen operating in European, Latin American and many African and Asian countries due to colonial expansion. Interestingly, Scotland operates a mixed common- and civil-law system.

Civilian law systems rely on codified laws and derive originally from Roman law. Civil law follows the group of legal ideas and systems stemming from the Roman-law Code of Justinian in France (and the French legal system is also strongly influenced by the Codes of Napoleon). However the civil-law system is also strongly overlaid by Germanic, ecclesiastical, feudal and generally learned, university and local practices, as well as doctrinal strains such as natural law, codification and legislative positivism (Lloyd, 1981, p. 275).

Civil law proceeds from abstractions, formulates general principles and distinguishes substantive rules from procedural rules. The legal profession relies closely on learned commentaries and articles that offer exposition on legal principles, although this has changed in more recent times, with civil-law jurisdictions relying more on reported judicial decisions as authoritative (Lloyd, 1981).

But statute or 'code' laws are the primary source of law. The court system is predominantly inquisitorial, not bound to follow precedent, and composed of specially trained judicial officers with a limited authority to interpret law. The core purpose of codified civil law is that it enables lawyers to interpret the law for and by themselves, rather than being dependent on judge-made, common-law precedents.

Juries do not make decisions separate from the judges, as in common-law systems, but in certain situations volunteer lay judges will participate along with legally trained career judges. Lay justices with minimal legal training but assisted by a legal clerk also work in common-law magistrate courts in the UK (Robertson and Nicol, 2008, p. 414).

As with common-law systems, there is a high degree of independence from the executive branch of government. However, an important difference setting civil-law systems apart from common-law systems is that the former emphasize the obligations of citizens, as distinct from simply setting out the range of prohibited conduct.

Socialist Law

In socialist legal systems the authority of the Communist ruling party overrides the authority of courts. It is based on the civil-law system, with major modifications and additions from Marxist-Leninist frameworks. Examples include China, the Russian Federation and North Korea.

The actual processes and application of the law will vary by country, but in China for example, 'anything which harms the morality of society or negates respected cultural traditions', as well as publications that 'deny the need for society to be guided by Marxism, Leninism, the system of thought of Mao Zedong' are prohibited (Wang and Davis, 2006, in Crook, 2010).

Due to overarching control of the legal system in China by the ruling Chinese Communist party (CCP), most courts are closed to the public/citizens, or any other kind of external scrutiny. In recent times, broad economic trends of marketization have introduced further layers of complexity into the Chinese socialist legal system. Since the media tend to be very closely guided by the party, there are strict controls over media content, which is supervised on a daily basis. This means that in practice, journalists and media publishers need to conform to restrictions placed by the CCP on specific lists of prohibited publications and restricted topics. In an era of rapid economic reform in China, McGregor argues that legal intellectuals 'increasingly have the ear of the leadership, which publicly espouses support for harmonizing Chinese legislation with global standards' (McGregor, 2010, p. 23). The overwhelming presence of the party can be further seen in the number of lawyers who are CCP members. According to McGregor, 'about one-third, or 45,000 of the 150,000 registered lawyers in China as of May 2009, were party members'. The entrenchment of the CCP in the wider legal system can be gauged by his observation that

> nearly all law firms, about 95%, had party committees, which assessed lawyers' pay not just according to their legal work, but to their party loyalty as well. Far from being a weakness, the party considers its penetration of the legal system to be a core strength.
>
> (ibid.)

Despite trends towards a more open society, Western ideals of the 'rule of law', as discussed in Chapter 1, have gained little traction, as seen, for example, in the infuriated reaction of the Chinese leadership to the awarding of the Nobel Peace Prize to democracy activist and literary critic, Liu Xiaobo. Liu was involved in the Tiananmen Square demonstrations in 1989, and more recently became one of the founders of the reform group Charter 08. At the time of the ceremony Liu was still imprisoned, having been so since December 2009, on a charge of subversion for co-authoring the Charter 08 document, and unable to attend and collect his prize money of $US 1.4 million (BBC News, 2010). It was reported that during the prize-giving in Oslo, Norway, both CNN and BBC TV channels in China, went black for the duration of the ceremony.

Islamic Law

This is a much older system than the other contemporary world legal systems discussed so far. Islam, like Christianity and other monotheistic religions, is often complex and interpretations of it vary. Islamic-law legal systems operate in Saudi Arabia, Iran, some Northern African and South East Asian countries.

These Muslim states can be said to be using classical Sharia law. Interestingly, the term *Shari'a* is from the Arabic word 'path' or 'way', based on the teachings of the Prophet Mohammed and beyond those, one God or Allah. In this way it shares links with other religious and philosophical traditions of thought such as Confucianism and 'Daoist' traditions based on a path/way. The result is that, for example, Saudi Arabia and other Gulf states do not have constitutions or legislatures. Their rulers have limited authority to change laws, since they are based on Sharia, as interpreted by their religious scholars. Iran shares some of these characteristics, but it has a parliament that legislates in a manner consistent with Sharia law. Islamic law derives from two main sources: *Shari'a* and *Sunnah*, which correspond to the main religious groupings within Islam itself.

Saudi and Iranian law relies on the Qur'an, which governs the relationship between citizen and legal system. Interpretation is undertaken by clerics rather than secular leaders or officials, 'judges' have only a secondary role. Crook argues that this may explain why 'the doctrine of *Siyyasa Shar'yya*, a discretionary interpretation of Islamic law in the public interest, has not led to a wider or more noticeable imitation of Western laws and standards in human rights and media freedom' (Crook, 2010, p. 345). Decisions of the Saudi Arabia's highest court, the Supreme Judicial Council (SJC) *and* the King, retain the power of final judgment, with no opportunity to review this exercise of power.

Sharia law deals with many topics present in secular legal systems, including crime, politics and economics, but to these we can add personal matters such as sexuality, hygiene, diet, prayer and fasting. In fact, Islamic law covers both civil and criminal justice, in addition to regulating individual conduct that is both personal and moral. The custom-based body of law, then, is based on the Qu'ran and the religion of Islam. Because, by definition, Muslim states are theocracies, religious texts are the law, the latter distinguished by Islam and Muslims in their application, as Sharia or Sharia law.

However, we need to be aware that there is complexity in the genres of Sharia as they are manifested in different nation-states. For example, some Muslim states have declared themselves to be secular: in this category we have Mali, Kazakhstan and Turkish states, where religious interference in state affairs, law and politics is prohibited. In these Muslim countries, the role of Sharia law, as in the secular West, is limited to personal and family matters (Badr, 1978).

There are Muslim states with hybrid sources of law: Pakistan, Indonesia, Afghanistan, Egypt, Nigeria, Sudan, Morocco and Malaysia have legal systems strongly influenced by Sharia, but they also draw ultimate authority from their constitutions and the rule of law. These countries conduct democratic elections, although some are also under the influence of authoritarian leaders and politicians and jurists make law, rather than religious scholars. Most of these countries have modernized their laws and now have legal systems with significant differences when compared to classical Sharia.

In general though, law is subordinate to religion in Islamic law. Courts are closed, although some punitive processes occur in public spaces. As in China, those media practitioners working within Islamic legal systems who report on what in the West would be seen as infringements of human rights are likely to be singled out for very punitive treatments.

From a Western perspective there will often be considerable differences between liberal democratic social practices that are considered to be reasonably addressed under the law. A glaring example would be the treatment of women deemed to have offended against sexual mores, where they may receive very harsh penalties, even death by public stoning, in certain circumstances. Predictably, these kinds of events are reported in highly judgmental terms by Western media, while other more moderate events illustrating comparable systemic elements are dismissed as 'unnewsworthy'. In a gesture of legal pluralism, the Archbishop of Canterbury, Rowan Williams has called for the 'constructive accommodation' of parts of Sharia law in the UK. The Australian Federation of Islamic Councils has made a similar suggestion in Australia. But right-wing critics decry such moves, insisting that they represent 'grave risks', have 'no place in a liberal model of multiculturalism' and cautioning that 'there must be limits to diversity' (Soutphommasane, 2011).

Common Law Systems in Further Detail

In this section we will consider some fundamental features of the common-law legal system in further detail. There are often approximate equivalents in the other legal systems we have discussed, but here the focus is on common-law legal systems.

The Courts

Knowledge of the court hierarchy and the jurisdiction of particular courts can assist journalists and other media practitioners in assessing the general significance of a case.

The highest appeal court in the UK and Wales is the Supreme Court, a role formerly held by the House of Lords until the passing of the Constitutional Reform Act 2005. The Judicial Committee of Privy Council is the court of final appeal for the UK overseas territories and Crown dependencies, and for those Commonwealth countries that have retained the appeal to Her Majesty in Council. In the Australian legal system it is the High Court of Australia. In the US it is the Supreme Court. The role of the highest courts is to interpret the constitution and to hear appeals from other courts in the hierarchy. As the highest court in Australia, decisions of the High Court are binding on all other Australian courts. This pattern is repeated in other Westminster-style models, as found in, for example, Canada, New Zealand, Hong Kong or Malaysia.

Different courts have varying jurisdictions. For example, in Australia, freedom-of-expression cases, which are heard in the High Court, are of great interest to media practitioners.

The term 'jurisdiction' has two main meanings:

1   the power granted to a legal body, such as a court or tribunal, to administer justice within a defined area of responsibility; or
2   a geographically delimited area within which certain laws are seen to apply (for example, a state, territory or nation).

Next in the Australian court hierarchy is the Federal Court, which has original and appellate jurisdiction. The states and territories also have their own courts, which interpret and apply the law. In ascending tiers, these are:

- *Magistrates' Courts*, which deal with the most common criminal offences such as traffic infringements and minor assaults, and smaller civil claims such as debt recovery.
- *Intermediate Courts*, such as District or County Courts, which hear the majority of serious criminal offences (often with a jury) and more serious civil claims up to certain monetary limits.
- *Supreme Courts*, which are the highest courts in Australian states and territories, and deal with the most serious criminal and civil claims. These courts may sit with either a single judge, or a 'bench' of three judges as an appeal or 'full' court to hear appeals from decisions made by judges in courts or tribunals lower in the hierarchy. Supreme Courts usually have specific categories or 'lists' of matters they can hear; for example, defamation cases (on the 'Defamation List') are heard at this level.

The Court hierarchy in England and Wales needs to be situated within the wider context of the European Union. In ascending tiers, these are:

- *Magistrates' Courts*, with a civil jurisdiction, deal with family proceedings, less serious criminal and youth court jurisdictions.
- *County Courts* deal with more serious civil cases, small claims, family proceedings, patents.
- *Crown Court* for serious appealable criminal matters, jury trials of indictable offences, appeals from magistrates' courts on fact and sentence.
- *Divisional Courts* have both civil and criminal jurisdictions, and may deal with appeals from bankruptcy, magistrates' and crown courts.
- *High Court* has Chancery, Family and Queen's Bench Divisions.
- *Court of Appeal* has a civil division, examining appeals of general public importance and a criminal division.
- *Supreme Court* hears appeals from Court of Appeal and High Court.
- *European Courts of Human Rights* treats advisory opinions or rulings against member states. The European Court of Justice hears actions against member states.

(Crook, 2010, pp. 62–4)

Sources of Law

As noted, there are two principal sources of law: statute law and common law. The former refers to laws enacted by state or federal parliaments, while the latter refers to judge-made law as decided in specific cases over time and through the interpretation of statutes; together, these are known as the 'doctrine of precedent'. The mechanism of 'precedent', then, is a feature of common-law systems.

Since common-law systems derive from the English legal system, they are followed mostly in those countries with a previous colonial connection to England, such as Australia, Canada, New Zealand and the US. The application of the common-law system diverges in the US from other former colonies as a result of its system being shaped by a powerfully independent Congress and Supreme Court. However, in all common-law-system countries the outcome of cases can be uncertain, depending on the interpretation of the legislation and the relevance of judgments in previous cases. Parliaments may change legislation at any time, and judges must work within the current Acts and rules of statutory interpretation.

The common-law system is often contrasted with civilian-law systems existing in much of Europe, and their interpretation of statutory codes.

Civil and Criminal Cases

Media practitioners might be parties to criminal or civil actions, depending on the nature of the published material. Criminal actions are brought by the state. A driver who breaks the speed limit knows there is a risk of encountering the criminal-justice system. Likewise, a publisher who interferes with the business of the courts might face criminal charges. By contrast, civil actions occur when legal proceedings are commenced by private individuals or entities, to obtain compensation or redress, from those who they claim have caused them harm. If a media publisher is responsible for material that impugns the reputation of a person, then they may well be sued under defamation law for the hurt and pain caused.

One major difference is that in criminal cases, the accused is presumed innocent until a court finds otherwise. In civil cases, however, there is usually no notion of 'guilt' or 'innocence', in the criminal sense. The plaintiff attempts to obtain some kind of remedy for the perceived wrongdoing, and a court might award damages.

A further difference may be illustrated by way of an example. In 2005, a high-profile community leader, Mr X, faced rape charges. The Crown lost the case on the evidence before the court. Mr X was therefore found by the court to be innocent of the rape charges. The following year, a woman claiming to be the victim in that same rape case sued Mr X in a civil action for damages, and won. Guilt in a criminal case must be proven 'beyond reasonable doubt', but in a civil action, the evidence is sifted through and a case is won or lost 'on the balance of probabilities'.

All parties to a legal action have rights and obligations. The fundamental right – of great interest to writers, playwrights, novelists, musicians, performers, producers, publishers and other media workers – is that to freedom of expression. In essence freedom of expression for media practitioners refers to the fundamental legal right to discover important information and convey it to the public.

Without this freedom, the law can impinge on the efforts of media to report important information and ideas to the public. First in the newsroom, and then in the courts, we see the tensions between the right to freedom of expression and other rights and freedoms. Such rights include the right to a good reputation (defamation laws), the right to a fair trial (contempt laws), the right to safeguard secrets (confidential-information laws), the right to privacy (laws protecting personal information and communications), and the right to protect our intellectual and creative property (intellectual property laws, including copyright).

In the newsroom, a team of editorial staff – including the journalist, the editor, possibly a legal advisor and sometimes the executive manager or proprietor – may all have advice regarding the constraints of the law.

Predicting the exact extent of freedoms for media practitioners is not always clear-cut, and this is why the media take a special interest in cases that may have implications for future media practice. When a case is before a court, one party will be arguing for the freedom to publish; the other for restrictions on publication, for redress or for compensation, because the publication may have harmed the plaintiff in some way. The role of the court is to tease out all the available evidence, interpreting the circumstances according to the relevant legislation and previous case law.

Traditions of Free Speech

In the US, freedom of the press is called the 'first freedom': free speech and freedom of the press were written into the US Constitution from its inception. In Australia there is no absolute right to free speech and no federal bill of rights guaranteeing free speech. However, we should recognize that in all common-law democracies, speech is always fettered by certain laws, practices, cultural traditions and habits.

In the UK, despite being a country without a written constitution, there is a rich history of, at least in rhetoric, free speech. Although Article 10 of the European Convention of Human Rights, guaranteeing free expression, was incorporated into British law with the enactment of the Human Rights Act, it's been argued that free expression 'has never been at home in Britain' (Robertson and Nicol, 2008, p. 2).

It was ironic, then, that English liberal ideals from Locke, Paine, Milton, Bentham and Mill informed the writing of the American Declaration of Independence in 1776, the US Constitution in 1789 and the Bill of Rights in 1791 (Crook, 2010, p. 5). The First Amendment to the US Constitution left the media in a position to act more freely than the British media would ever be able to. But even in the US, there has been a litany of high-profile battles fought contradicting the presumption of an unalloyed right to free expression in the media; from the McCarthyist media witch hunts of Communists in the Cold War period; to the Pentagon Papers (when the *New York Times* progressively published leaked Vietnam War dossiers); to Watergate and the impeachment of President Nixon; the Plame Affair (involving the leaking of confidential CIA information about Iraq to the media); through to the questioning of the role of the *New York Times* by the US administration in WikiLeaks' Cablegate.

We can therefore observe that quite specific cultural traditions operate in these Anglophone common-law jurisdictions. For example, Australia is a signatory to the UN's 1948 Universal Declaration of Human Rights, the International Covenant on Civil and Political Rights, and the International Covenant on Economic, Social and Cultural Rights, which protect limited rights, and the High Court of Australia has ruled on several occasions since 1971 that there is an implied constitutional freedom of expression in political and government matters (Beattie and Beal, 2007, ch. 5). Australian law, then, has a tradition of freedom of expression, even though it has no constitutional bill of rights. In general terms, we can define a bill of rights as legislation, through parliament or a clause in the constitution, that guarantees citizens a legal right to certain freedoms. In Australia, only the Australian Capital Territory (Human Rights Act 2004) and the state of Victoria (Human Rights and Responsibilities Act 2006) have enacted their own charters of human rights.

To understand the evolution of freedom of speech, it is helpful to trace events back more than 500 years. Even before the development of the printing press in the fifteenth century, powerful people feared the spoken word. Death, imprisonment and mutilation were punishments for the spreading of gossip. How much more fear would the written word create among the nobility, when they realised the damage a free press could do to their reputations? In the seventeenth century John Milton made his speech in parliament in defence of free speech and a free press, 'A Speech for the Liberty of Unlicensed Publishing', later published as the *Areopagitica* (Butler and Rodrick 2007, p. 4). The law of treason may have been in slow decline along with the absolute powers of monarchy, but the lineage of laws of sedition and 'seditious libel' flows right through to present-day Australia. Amendments to Commonwealth sedition laws were enacted through Schedule 7 of the Anti-Terrorism Act (No 2) 2005 (Cth). This development should be illustration enough that the idea of 'freedom of speech' is a matter that ultimately depends on specific, historically contingent expressions of power within a particular jurisdiction.

It was only in 2009 that the UK parliament set the world-leading example by abolishing its ancient anti-speech laws of sedition and criminal libel. These offences dated from the time of the Star Chamber and were used in 1792 against Thomas Paine on the ground that the *Rights of Man* brought into hatred and contempt the sovereign, parliament, kingdom, constitution, laws and government. An act of sedition is one that incites hatred or contempt for the Crown, government or constitution. It is widely cast: sedition is any act done or word spoken or written and published which has a 'seditious tendency' or done, spoken or written and published with a 'seditious intent'.

Announcing their abolition, Lord Bach noted: 'Sedition and defamatory libel are arcane offences from a bygone era when freedom of expression wasn't seen as the right it is today' (Gibb, 2009). The move followed earlier recommendations for reform by the Law Commission in 1977 and 1985 and, prior to their abolition, a campaign by a coalition of writers, actors, lawyers, entertainers and politicians, as well as pressure from the rights activist groups Index on Censorship, Liberty, English PEN and Article 19.

Free speech has been philosophically justified in relation to arguments linking it to individual autonomy and liberties, famously invoked by John Stuart Mill's essay 'On Liberty' (1859), in addition to arguments underpinned by the fundamental debates about the value of 'truth' and 'democracy'. It should be clear that debates about the media and the role of media practitioners in the public sphere are closely connected with these wider, historically rich, debates in liberal democracies.

As Beattie and Beal note:

> From their earliest inception these rights had a public character, protecting public assembly and distribution of information, and a private character, protecting individual communications from state scrutiny and keeping the state out of private spaces. The spatial nature of these rights influences the ways in which broadcasting and communications are regulated today.
>
> (2007, p. 89)

As democracies have evolved, so too has a recognition of human rights, among them the right to hold and express a view, particularly a view about those people in government who represent the citizens.

Arguing for the democratic merits of a written constitution that enshrines freedom of expression and of the media, John Keane makes the point that: 'A great variety of legal means can help to promote freedom of expression and access to information among transacting citizens' (Keane, 1991, p. 128). Publication through the media is the key vehicle by which citizens exercise this right to express their views in the public sphere.

Tolerance and Vilification

Democratic governments, to a greater or lesser extent, tolerate a range of views, including those many might disagree with. Famously, the French philosopher Voltaire described freedom of speech in these terms: 'I disapprove of what you say, but I will defend to the death your right to say it.' The argument being that in the tolerance of all views, even false ones, the truth will emerge, in bits and pieces perhaps, dispersed, and variously revealed, but eventually it will shine through, and this is the incontrovertible quality of freedom of expression.

Taking a long view of the development of free speech, it can be argued that there has been a general shift in focus away from individual political figures, towards the regulation of 'dangerous speech' (Beattie and Beal, 2007, p. 89). Such speech includes vilification or hate speech. Anti-vilification laws are in conflict with the concept of free speech and are justified on the basis of an overriding public interest. In Australia, these laws use an anti-discrimination model and are regulated at state and federal level through anti-discrimination agencies like the Human Rights and Equal Opportunity Commission, which relies on the Racial Hatred Act 1995 (Cth) to operate a complaints-based scheme. If unsuccessful, conciliation is supported by other remedies, including the application of monetary penalties (ibid., p. 99).

Arguably, to suppress one view, which we might believe to be false and damaging, is to risk suppressing worthy views closer to the truth. Furthermore, any suppression of views raises the question: who shall have the right to exercise this control? Governments and other powerful institutions that suppress freedom of speech, such as courts, are frequently in conflict with the media. Journalists, and often courts too, hold very strongly to the principle of freedom of expression, though the relationship is perennially unsettled. Consider the events listed below, which were widely reported by the media.

- A Danish newspaper, the *Jyllands-Posten*, published cartoons of the Prophet Mohammed carrying a suicide bomb in his turban. Many lives were lost in the violent civil protests following their publication.
- The British historian David Irving was jailed in Austria for denying aspects of the mid-twentieth-century Holocaust in Europe.
- The Australian historian Keith Windschuttle disputed historical accounts of mass killings of indigenous Australians in colonial times.

These ideas are unpalatable to many, because they are either false, offensive, unsubstantiated or highly contentious. It is also possible to make distinctions between cartoons and ideas that are expressed in other media forms and genres, and the size and location of the audiences that listen, watch or read them. But advocates for free speech say it is better to discuss such views publicly than to suppress them, for public discussion takes all citizens closer to the truth by fostering the emergence of strong reasoning and vital debate, which energize democracy.

It is important that media practitioners become familiar with the jurisdictions in which they work. Even within particular countries, differences might apply between the states, which have their own legislatures. Democracies themselves vary significantly in the legal guarantees for publishers. Yet even though legal systems vary from one jurisdiction to another, these principles warrant ongoing discussion. Armed with the foregoing information, we can now consider some specific laws relevant to media practitioners in their daily work.

Contempt of Court

A key area of concern for media practitioners who report the courts, or who make any media product referencing actual events that may also be judicially considered, is the legal principle of contempt of court. Contempt laws aim to ensure that the justice system works fairly for all citizens. They form a subset of the wider idea of the rule of law discussed in Chapter 1. Four principles underpin contempt laws in common-law legal systems:

1 open justice;
2 the right to a fair trial;
3 the presumption of innocence;
4 public confidence in the legal system.

Beyond these principles is the idea that justice must not only be done, but must be seen to be done. Hence any publication with the potential to damage a fair trial could lead to a contempt charge. With this in mind, media practitioners in general, and journalists in particular, need to tread carefully when presenting content about matters relating to the courts. Contempt of court is usually a criminal offence, most typically punishable by a fine or prison sentence. In essence, contempt of court can be defined as any conduct which interferes with, or has the potential to interfere with, the administration of justice in general, or in particular, to damage a fair trial.

The media is prohibited from reporting material from a closed court, or from proceedings that are subject to suppression orders. Generally this is 'in the interests of the administration of justice', for instance, to protect witnesses, to facilitate police informers coming forward to give evidence and to safeguard the rights of the accused to a fair trial.

In broad terms, in Australia there have traditionally been three categories of contempt laws: 'contempt in the face of court', where a person offends or otherwise behaves badly within a court; 'scandalizing the court', where a person offends the court while outside the court, for example through publication; and most importantly, *sub judice* contempt laws, which attempt to prevent 'trial by media' and the impact media coverage may have on swaying the views of jurors. It is the latter that is arguably the most frequently concerning for media practitioners. As it is usually a criminal matter, a person who has committed a contempt and been found guilty will have this criminal conviction recorded. There are specific contempt laws for particular courts: for family courts, children's courts, parliaments and commissions of inquiry, including standing commissions against corruption and crime.

There are variations between jurisdictions in common-law systems in relation to the precise application and local interpretations of contempt laws. In the UK, the Contempt of Court Act 1981 deals with a wide range of mostly 'strict liability contempt' (where intentionality plays no part), and it expressly allows for all other common-law variants of contempt. In the US, the approach is set apart from many other jurisdictions by its stronger focus on First Amendment priorities of freedom of speech in media reporting and coverage of criminal trials. Crook suggests that British jurisprudence 'constantly avers' to a 1913 decision by the House of Lords in *Scott* v. *Scott* ([1913] AC 417). Over the subsequent century the rubicon of open justice was 'crossed on very rare occasions' (Crook, 2010). Pre-mass electronic media, the divorce case extolled the virtues of the open conduct of trials, and indeed has been referred to as 'the leading modern authority on the principle of open justice' (Rolph *et al.*, 2010, p. 401). A ban on sketching and the use of cameras became law in 1925/6; in 1933 parliament gave judges discretionary powers to prohibit the naming of juvenile witnesses and defendants; and judges gave themselves powers to conceal the identity of homosexual victims of blackmail gangs. The latter development led in 1974 to Chief Justice Widgery in the case of *R* v. *Paul Foot and Socialist Worker* formalizing a common-law right to anonymity for blackmail complainants. Paul Foot was a legendary investigative journalist who was seeking to expose the use of a brothel by members of the British establishment, but did not wish to compromise national security (Crook, 2010, p. 273).

After the Contempt of Court Act 1981 was introduced, the power to order prior restraint and prohibit reporting by the media of criminal cases was formalized. For Crook a 'media and the courts' battlefield worth hundreds of millions of pounds in litigation has ensued. The battlelines are drawn between freedom of expression, a right to a fair trial, to privacy and life and concerns over national security. Goldberg *et al.* (2009) suggest that following the defeat of the UK in the European Court of Human Rights in the Thalidomide case, the Contempt of Court Act ushered in a new period of liberalization for the media. The *Sunday Times* had published an article bringing to public notice the responsibility of the manufacturers of the drug Thalidomide for the victims of birth defects. On appeal, the UK House of Lords restored an injunction restraining publication. The Court of Human Rights in Strasbourg decided that the injunction restricted the freedom of expression of the *Sunday Times* (ibid., p. 98).

Sub Judice *Contempt*

The two main ways in which media may be in contempt of court are by publishing material that could influence a trial and by disobeying a court order. A 'strict liability rule' applies to conduct which tends to interfere with particular legal proceedings, and which in practice creates a substantial risk of prejudice or impeding a case.

The right to a fair trial, uninterrupted by the media, is highly valued in Western democracies. Equally, as former Australian High Court Justice Michael McHugh has argued, 'The publication of fair and accurate reports of court proceedings is vital to the proper working of an open and democratic society and to the maintenance of public confidence in the administration of justice' (*Fairfax* v. *Police Tribunal of NSW*

[1986] 5 NSWLR 465). The cost to society of trial by media can be high: delays and even acquittals can result, denying citizens justice as a consequence. Defence lawyers can also use prejudicial publications to their own advantage, arguing that their client could not receive a fair trial after media coverage.

Media practitioners, and particularly journalists reporting courts need to be aware that there are strict rules about what can be reported while proceedings are 'active'. Publications relating to a trial – when that trial is pending (or, 'imminent') or under way – are called *sub judice* publications. Judicial 'activity' in itself does not preclude media reporting if it does not pose 'a substantial risk of serious prejudice' (Robertson and Nicol, 2008, p. 426).

We can divide the *sub judice* period into several 'time zones' for criminal trials. The first is the period after a crime has been committed, before an arrest warrant has been issued. This is a safe time to interview witnesses and police.

The second time zone, in criminal proceedings, commences when a summons to appear or warrant for arrest is issued, or another document specifying the charge. In Scotland, an oral charge is sufficient to activate proceedings (Goldberg *et al.*, 2009, p. 100). This is a danger period for the media, because it's difficult to know when the situation develops from 'assisting the police with their inquiries' to the laying of charges. At this time when proceedings are active, the media may only report bare facts of the issuing of the summons or warrant and arrest but not details of the person.

Third, there is a period of time between charges being laid and the commencement of the trial. Proceedings are not 'pending' just because police inquiries are under way. (In civil proceedings, 'pending' in this sense refers to the period from the issuing of a writ or statement of claim or summons, and the setting of a trial date, up until the commencement of the trial.) During this time, the known details of the person can be published, and any details that emerge in open court.

Technically, the *sub judice* period, while a trial is pending or under way, is when heavy restrictions are placed on the release of information about the trial. During this period, journalists can report the charges and can identify the accused or respondents/defendants, provided the charges do not involve children as victims or accused. Information that presumes guilt or innocence, that refers to any past (or 'spent') convictions, or might be relevant to the case, is prohibited.

The next stage of the *sub judice* period is the trial itself, when journalists can report anything stated in an open court, as long as it is fair and accurate. In cases before a jury more care needs to be taken in reporting the proceedings than in cases before a judge alone, as jurors are considered to be more susceptible to outside 'influence' than a judge.

There is also a period after the trial has concluded, but before the expiration of the date for lodging an appeal. Care needs to be exercised at this time, but once the time has lapsed, it will then be safe to speak with witnesses but not jurors in many jurisdictions. Similarly, once a person is acquitted, or found guilty and sentenced, the media are on safer ground.

Children's courts are closed, not reportable, and identities of all participants are protected. Breaches of the law relating to children's courts are extremely serious.

We can see now how the law relating to *sub judice* publications might impinge on freedom of expression. Imagine you have witnessed a robbery, assault or some other crime. The police charge someone within hours. You know the person committed the act because you saw the event, but you cannot publish this fact in the *sub judice* period. It is the courts alone that decide the facts, not the media. It is easy to get a sense of this process if you put yourself in the shoes of an accused person: you would expect a fair trial through proper court processes rather than trial by media, wouldn't you?

The *sub judice* laws in relation to civil matters are not as strict, since the standard of proof ('on the balance of probabilities' not 'beyond reasonable doubt') is not as onerous; there is no concern about jurors being 'influenced'; and a person's liberty is not on the line. All citizens are entitled to the rule of law and to the presumption of innocence until a proper court process finds otherwise. Presumption of innocence refers to the right of an accused person to innocence in law until convicted by a court.

The media have remarkable power to influence the fairness of this process, and this explains why courts so readily issue a 'suppression order' prohibiting publication, even to an excessive extent, in some jurisdictions (Kenyon, 2006, 2007).

The terms of suppression orders or injunctions can at times be overly restrictive. In the highly publicized Trafigura case in 2009, Mr Justice Maddison granted a so-called 'super injunction' to restrain the *Guardian* newspaper from publishing details of a report commissioned by the oil-trading company Trafigura, about illegal dumping which involved fifteen deaths. The terms of the injunction prohibited the *Guardian* from revealing that an injunction had been granted to Trafigura, and even from reporting parliamentary debates discussing the injunction (Davies, 2009 in Pearson and Polden, 2011, pp. 90–1).

The event triggered a media storm when Trafigura's lawyers wrote to the Speaker of the House of Commons, arguing that the issue was *sub judice*, on the basis that a class action for the victims was in play, and libel (defamation) actions were also under way against the BBC (Booth, 2009). The Speaker of the House urged that there was a need to robustly defend freedom of speech in parliament. MP Paul Farrelly was reported at the time as saying

> Firstly they tried and failed to suppress news that they had obtained a gagging order against the *Guardian*. Then they tried to ask the Speaker to gag parliament itself. This affair has shown us that privileges protecting press freedom are sometimes only as strong as their assertion.
>
> (ibid.)

The debate in the House proceeded and details emerged on social-networking sites, and this led Trafigura to partially release the injunction.

Notorious cases often result in breaches of contempt laws. So frenzied might the media pack and the public be for information that the courts are sometimes powerless to stop abuses of the justice process. In December 2006, police in England charged a man with the murder of five prostitutes in what became known as the 'Suffolk Strangler' case (Troup, 2006). Although public discussion must cease after a suspect is charged, *The Sun* newspaper published prejudicial material, including a photograph of the accused mock-strangling his former wife, and quotes from two prostitutes alleging he had cruised for sex dressed in drag. Police and the Attorney-General reprimanded the media for threatening the man's right to a fair trial.

Publications in other jurisdictions are usually harder to contain. A court has power only over its own state, territory or nation, and this explains why details of trials during the *sub judice* period might be published in another country. The trial in Australia of the murdered British backpacker Peter Falconio and his relationship with his girlfriend Joanne Lees (later to be gruesomely fictionalized in the film *Wolf Creek*), for example, were grist to the mill for the UK's tabloid media, while proceedings were *sub judice* in the Northern Territory.

The magazine *Who Weekly* experienced the heavy cost of *sub judice* contempt in 1994 in relation to the so-called 'backpacker murders' in New South Wales. *Who Weekly* published an image of the accused, Ivan

Milat, during the *sub judice* period, before his conviction. In the Milat case, the issue of identity was crucial to the trial, and in any event the publication of a photograph of an accused person is prohibited. The frontcover of the magazine carried the words: 'Backpacker serial killings. The accused. The private life of road worker Ivan Milat, the man charged with slaying 7 hitchhikers, as told by his brother Wally.' The magazine was fined AUS$100,000 and the editor AUS$10,000. The Court of Appeal found that the publisher had a right to seek profit from providing information as entertainment, but had no right to do so at the expense of the administration of justice (*Attorney-General for New South Wales v. Time Inc.*).

Defences to Sub Judice Contempt

A journalist charged with contempt of court has few defences, with truth not being among them. To understand why, return for a moment to the crime you have witnessed. Let's say you published the truth, that the accused committed the offence. But the case is *sub judice*, and your report has the potential to influence the jury, whose members must be free to decide their verdict on the basis of what goes before the court, not what they read or have the potential to read, see or hear in the media.

The main common-law defence for contempt of court is that of a fair and accurate report under qualified privilege. (There is a statutory version in section 5 of the UK's Contempt of Court Act 1981). Media practitioners may report exactly what was said in the court, and the 'bare facts' of the case, and if your report is a true and accurate account of those proceedings, you will have a defence.

There are wider public-interest defences which may apply, but they are usually a higher-risk proposition. The Australian broadcaster Derryn Hinch, a radio 'shock jock' relied on the public-interest argument when charged with contempt of court after referring on air to the prior convictions of a former priest, Michael Glennon, who was facing child sex offences in 1985. Hinch argued that the public had a right to know of the accused's history, but the court found that there was risk of serious prejudice to the trial because the statements might stay in the jurors' minds. Hinch repeated his on-air comments some months after the first occasion. At first instance, Judge Murphy fined Hinch AUS$25,000 and sentenced him to forty-two days' imprisonment. The Full Court of the Supreme Court of Victoria reduced the fine to AUS$15,000 and the sentence to twenty-eight days' imprisonment (*Hinch v. Attorney-General for the State of Victoria* [1987] 164 CLR 15). An important authority for a defence based on an overriding public interest is the judgment of Chief Justice Jordan in *Ex parte Bread Manufacturers Ltd; Re. Truth and Sportsman Ltd* in 1934. The case, concerning a discussion of collusive and anti-competitive practices in the baking industry, has been endorsed by the House of Lords and the High Court of Australia (Rolph *et al.*, 2010, p. 440).

Some Important Sub Judice Contempt Advice for Media Practitioners

Do not:

- state that a person is guilty or innocent before they have been convicted or acquitted;
- if reporting on a civil action, say a person is liable or negligent before a judgment is given;
- publish an admission of guilt outside the court process;
- publish the criminal record of the accused;
- publish confessions;
- publish evidence relating to the case;
- publish any independent investigation of the case;
- publish any statement in court when the jury is out of the court;
- publish a photograph of an accused person;
- publish a statement of a witness (or potential witness);
- pressure anyone not to participate in a case;
- publish that a trial is a retrial until the retrial is concluded.

There are a number of mitigating 'influence' factors that a court will take into account in weighing up publication contempt, including: the scope of circulation; proximity to trial; the venue of the trial (how much interest will it attract?); the memorable facts in the case – what is the 'fade factor'; sensationalism in the coverage; identification and images of accused; celebrity status and the existing notoriety of a person; and perhaps of most significance, previous convictions and character assessments (Goldberg *et al.*, 2009, pp. 107–17).

Statutory defences under the UK's Contempt of Court Act 1981 provide exceptions to the strict liability rule, for example, if the publisher was unaware after 'all reasonable care' was taken that proceedings were not active. However, this is a rare defence and difficult to prove in practice.

New Media and the Courts

In Australia an extensively publicized trial in early 2008, which became a widely discussed 'water-cooler' topic, occurred when the commercial free-to-air Nine Network was ordered by the Supreme Court in Victoria not to broadcast specific episodes of the television crime-drama series *Underbelly*. This court's decision was made on the basis that the material (referencing Melbourne's gangland murder subculture) would interfere with criminal proceedings in that state (*R* v. *[A]* [2008] VSC 73). Controversially, the judge's suppression orders also prohibited the series being viewed over the internet; a measure which, together with the fact that bootleg DVD copies were easily available, was very publicly seen as unenforceable and was widely discussed in the media.

Subsequent series of the drama experienced continuing legal difficulties arising from the programmes' connection to real people and events, and a general tendency to represent a 'trial by media'.

It has been suggested that the Court of Appeal's judgment in *General Television Corporation Pty Ltd* v. *Director of Public Prosecutions* has now 'added to the list of categories where a court may derogate from open justice' (Rotstein, 2010, p. 110). The disjuncture between the longstanding rationale behind contempt laws and the ways in which audiences are now able to consume their favourite media products was apparent for all to see.

It is clear that there is considerable pressure for reform of contempt laws because of the impact of digital-media usage. This has been an unfolding story in all jurisdictions for over a decade. So far there have been varying responses in different legal systems. The question of how to deal with the impact of social-media applications such as Facebook and Twitter, and digital media in general, has been exercising the minds of many lawyers and politicians, as was evident in the Trafigura case. However, recent developments in the UK have seen the courts attempt to respond to the mounting pressure of new communications technologies and applications, and in particular, small mobile devices that can be taken into court with a view to reporting proceedings as they take place. The sheer popularity of internet and mobile telephony devices has meant that the objectives of many contempt laws have been rendered redundant, or in need of substantial amendment.

Examples of the disjuncture between what is possible in the digital era, and the lengths courts are going to in order to prevent jurors from accessing material that would potentially jeopardise an accused's fair trial are clearly visible. Judges routinely order the removal of online material discussing an accused person and victims. This occurs when judges issue blanket orders suppressing media outlets from publicizing any kind of commentary or discussion of cases before the courts.

And yet some judges have apparently given up even attempting to prevent jurors from accessing publicly prejudicial material because they recognize the futility in this course of action. The new media reality is that search engines and information sharing on social-networking platforms such as Facebook and Twitter, and a plethora of devices mean that the horse has already bolted. In 2011 in the UK, it was reported that the names of certain celebrities, who were claimed to have obtained gagging injunctions, and their alleged misdemeanours, were freely transmitted on Twitter. This is a fascinating development for the courts, which have traditionally been able to, often on behalf of the powerful and influential, 'suppress inconvenient truths and false-hoods' (Bowcott and Sabbagh, 2011). Predictably, these developments have reignited calls for a specific tort of privacy in the UK (see Chapter 4). In theory, the Attorney-General in the UK could initiate proceedings for breach of a court order in the public interest, but this is unlikely to occur because of the problematic question of whether or not Twitter is a 'publisher'. There are mixed views among legal practitioners about the merits or otherwise of suing individual Twitter account holders. At the time of these events, one lawyer expressed the view regarding specific tweets that 'if it is false it is libelous; if it is true it is contemptuous' (ibid.).

Taking another strategic approach to these new social-media developments for the courts, the aptly named Lord Judge, Lord Chief Justice of England and Wales, asserted that, if juries are to survive, the courts need to be able to prevent access to the internet during critical periods of a trial. In late 2010, he issued an Interim Practice Guidance for the 'Use of live text-based forms of communication (including Twitter) from court for the purposes of fair and accurate reporting'. The Interim Guidance has application to court proceedings open to the public 'and those parts of the proceedings which are not subject to reporting restrictions' (Judge, 2010). In a sense, these measures are addressing the side of the problem that is still within the power of the legal system.

'Live text-based' is language designed to catch a broad variety of social media, email and other forms of messaging communications. In issuing the Interim Practice Guidance the Lord Chief Justice earmarked his intention to consult with senior legal officialdom and other relevant parties such as the Press Complaints Commission. His comments placed these new media and communications developments squarely in the context of the rule of law, open justice, the public interest in knowing what takes place in courts. The Lord Chief Justice framed these cultural and technological developments in reporting as a balancing act between freedom of speech, the right to a fair trial and the statutory requirement of fair and accurate reports of legal proceedings. In other words, the framing is consistent with the prevailing discourse of legal governance involving judicial and media relations.

The perceived risks seen to arise from 'live text-based forms of communication' from courts are listed as risks from disruption to proceedings, to fairness and in relation to coaching witnesses. The Interim Practice Guidance observes that 'the features of Twitter, for example, to respond quickly in a reactive manner to a threaded commentary, or to "retweet" earlier comments are considered to be potentially risky characteristics' (ibid.). It is interesting to note that the very affordances seen to characterize new social media are, in a judicial context, a threat to the principles of the administration of justice.

The general principles invoked by the Interim Guidance include that judges have an overriding responsibility to ensure that proceedings are conducted consistently with the proper administration of justice and open justice, including fair and accurate reporting. It is intended that statutory and discretionary exceptions for the prohibition on photography and the making of sound recordings (which are generally absolute) should be at the discretion of the court. In general, the proposed rule is that there are no prohibitions on the use of live text-based communications in open court. However, whether these communications are permitted is at the discretion of the court. The court must be satisfied that there is no danger of interference to the administration of justice.

The presumption made in the Interim Guidance is that this kind of reporting is more likely to be undertaken by 'representatives of the media', but will not be permitted by the wider public, including 'citizen journalists'. A judge may withdraw permission at any time, and this will involve important, and inevitably, ethically informed decisions. Even if representatives of the media or other non-accredited categories of users of devices (bloggers, other commentators, students) are seated in a designated area of the court, it may prove to be difficult to interpret and enforce this requirement. These developments in reporting judicial processes on new media platforms point both to the

resilience on the part of courts in responding to changing media practice and to the contemporary interface of legal and media systems.

References

Badr, G. (1978) 'Islamic Law: Its Relation to Other Legal Systems', *American Journal of Comparative Law* vol. 26 no. 2, Spring.
BBC News (2010) ' "Liu Xiaobo Must Be Freed" – Nobel Prize Committee', 10 December, available at http://www.bbc.co.uk/news/world-asia-pacific-11966449.
Beattie, S. and E. Beal (2007) *Connect and Converge: Australian Media and Communications Law* (Melbourne: Oxford University Press).
Booth, R. (2009) 'MPs' Super-injunction Debate to Go Ahead', 18 October, online at *Guardian.co.uk*.
Bowcott, O. and D. Sabbagh (2011) 'Courts Foiled by Twitter Breaches', 11 May, online at *Guardian.co.uk*.
Butler, D. and S. Rodrick (2007) *Australian Media Law*, 3rd edn (Sydney: Lawbook Company).
Court of Appeal (1994) *Attorney General for New South Wales v. Time Inc.*, unreported, 21 October.
Crook, T. (2010) *Comparative Media Law and Ethics* (London: Routledge).
De Zengotita, T. (2005) *Mediated: How the Media Shape Your World* (London: Bloomsbury).
General Television Corporation Pty Ltd v. *Director of Public Prosecutions [citation]*.
Gibb, F. (2009) 'Arcane Laws of Sedition and Criminal Libel Scrapped', 15 July, online at Times online.co.uk.
Goldberg, D., G. Sutter and I. Walden (2009) (eds) *Media Law and Practice* (Oxford: Oxford University Press).
Judge, CJ (2010) *Lord Chief Justice of England and Wales, Interim Practice Guidance: The Use of Live Text-based Forms of Communication (Including Twitter) from Court for the Purposes of Fair and Accurate Reporting*, 20 December, online at http://www.supremecourt.gov.uk/docs/live-text-based-comms.pdf.
Keane, J. (1991) *The Media and Democracy* (Cambridge: Polity).
Kenyon, A. T. (2006) *Defamation: Comparative Law and Practice* (London: UCL Press).
Kenyon, A. T. (2007) 'Not Seeing Justice Done: Suppression Orders in Australian Law and Practice', *Adelaide Law Review* vol. 27 no. 2, pp. 279–310.
Lloyd, D. (1981) *The Idea of Law* (Harmondsworth: Penguin).
McGregor, R. (2010) *The Party: The Secret World of China's Communist Rulers* (London and New York: Allen Lane/Penguin).
Pearson, M. and M. Polden (2011) *The Journalist's Guide to Media Law*, 4th edn (Sydney: Allen and Unwin).
Robertson, G. and A. Nicol (2008) *Media Law*, 5th edn (London: Penguin).
Rolph, D., M. Vitins and J. Bannister (2010) *Media Law: Cases, Materials and Commentary* (Melbourne: Oxford University Press).

Rotstein, F. (2010) 'Chewing the Fat of a Soft Underbelly', *Media and Arts Law Review* vol. 15 no. 1, pp. 83–110.

Soutphommasane, T. (2011) 'Avoid the Hysteria but Reject Sharia', Inquirer, *Weekend Australian*, 21–2 May.

Troup, J. (2006) 'Strangler Suspect No 2 Charged, *TheSun.co.uk*, 22 December, online at http://www.thesun.co.uk/sol/homepage/news/article76647.ece.

3 Defamation and the Protection of Reputations

Many people's understanding of defamation laws is thrust upon them by controversial defamation cases that become high-profile news stories. Undeniably, the way in which reputations are frequently damaged by the media holds a sort of *schadenfreude* fascination for us all. And it is probably because powerful politicians, businesspeople and celebrities are grist to the mill of the news-media scandal-and-gossip machine that we tend to pay attention when these kinds of people use the defamation laws to seek compensatory damages. In essence, defamation laws, which evolved from a statute in the thirteenth century creating a criminal offence of *scandalum magnatum*, are concerned with balancing an individual's right to safeguard their reputation with a general right to exercise freedom of communication (Robertson and Nicol, 2008). But that first criminal-offence statute has set the tone over the subsequent centuries: its purpose was to protect 'the great men of the realm' from stories capable of turning the people against them. Several centuries later, the Star Chamber allowed noblemen to commence civil actions for libel, which may have been in some situations an alternative to duelling. For a media practitioner, it can be challenging to find deeper ethical principles in many of the defamation laws that operate today. Yet, it is precisely because of this complex balancing act that defamation laws represent an ethical discourse that reconfigures over time; in response to shifts in power and their attendant moralities within commercial, legal and political contexts. In this chapter we consider how defamation has evolved across different common-law jurisdictions, the fundamentals of defamation, key 'hotspots' that will assist in guiding media practitioners and the significant implications and consequences of using new media platforms.

Although defamation laws are usually relied on by the kinds of people you would expect to see, hear or read about in the media, in other circumstances, people who have had little or no previous exposure to the harsh glare of the media suddenly become the object of fascination. Who can forget the Madeleine McCann kidnapping and the subsequent media storm? In many ways it epitomized contemporary mainstream media, and the mediatization of symbolic content (Belnaves *et al.*, 2009, p. 4). When Madeleine McCann, aged just three, vanished from the apartment in Algarve, Portugal, in which her British parents had been staying, it instantly received global media coverage. Were her parents, Kate and Gerry McCann from Leicestershire in the UK, somehow responsible for her disappearance or was it a genuine kidnapping? Was Madeleine, as her parents claimed, abducted by a deranged kidnapper on 3 May 2007 while they dined out at a nearby restaurant in the complex where they were staying? Predictably, her parents were hounded 24/7 by the media, salivating at the prospect of scooping the worst-case scenario story. The notorious British tabloid press had a field day.

The Express Newspapers Group (UK), whose mastheads include the *Daily Express, Daily Star* and *Sunday Express*, paid £550,000 in damages to the Find Madeleine Fund for 100 articles published in the group's newspapers (BBC, 2008). The Express Group admitted it had been wrong to suggest in these articles that the McCanns were responsible for their daughter's death. The papers responsible also printed front-page apologies. The case, which began in the High Court of England and Wales, was settled and did not proceed to trial. This is in itself an interesting 'chilling' mechanism against free speech: a decision was made by the defendant's legal team that it would be economically more prudent to settle 'out of court' than to proceed to what in all likelihood would be a more expensive trial, with liability being incurred for legal costs for the plaintiffs and defendants, in the event of the defendants losing the case. The media commentator, now academic, Roy Greenslade, remarked at the time that 'for two national newspapers to carry front-page apologies at the same time was "unprecedented"' (ibid.).

Prior to reaching this settlement, Express titles had actually made news out of their own admissions of wrongdoing. They published one front-page story with the headline 'Kate and Gerry McCann: Sorry'. The *Daily Express* commented that a 'number of articles in the newspaper have suggested that the couple caused the death of their missing daughter Madeleine and then covered it up', acknowledging that there was 'no evidence whatsoever' to support this theory and adding that Kate and Gerry McCann were 'completely innocent of any involvement in their daughter's disappearance' (ibid.).

The website set up by the McCanns to help investigate Madeleine's disappearance informs us that 'over £1 million in libel damages and compensation awarded to Kate and Gerry McCann and their friends has been paid into Madeleine's Fund'. Clearly, the potential to gain financial compensation through legal action for damage to a person's reputation continues to be an important motivating factor for plaintiffs in this kind of litigation. In an endeavour to curb financial-damages abuses in Australia, as one of the outcomes of national reform of defamation laws in 2005/6, the quantum of financial damages was capped at AUS$250,000 (subject to regular indexed adjustments), although judges continue to have discretionary powers to go above this amount in specific circumstances. Before considering the practical rules of defamation (or libel) we should first look into the important jurisdictional background to these laws.

Defamation Laws

From a jurisprudential perspective there are clear divergences between Anglophone jurisdictions. One key difference is between the US jurisdiction, which favours freedom of speech, and defendants under the US Constitution, as compared with the UK jurisdiction, which has a strong tendency to favour a plaintiff's reputation when commencing defamation actions.

The First Amendment to the US Constitution provides that

> Congress shall make no law respecting an establishment of religion, or prohibiting the free exercise thereof; or abridging the freedom of speech, or of the press; or the right of the people peaceably to assemble, and to petition the government for a redress of grievances.

As a result of this provision, the US has a relatively freer media culture, and particularly so in relation to freedom of communication by media publishers. However, it is not an absolutist free-expression utopia, and there are many examples of the US legal system restricting various kinds of speech, not the least of which are defamation laws, even if the bar is set higher for defendants than in other common-law systems.

This 'constitutionalization' of defamation has arisen as a direct consequence of the foundational US Supreme Court libel-law decision in *New York Times Inc* v. *Sullivan*, 1964. In the context of the Civil Rights movement, activists had accused a public-affairs commissioner responsible for the police department in Montgomery, Alabama of failing to perform his duties to investigate racist attacks on Dr Martin Luther King and his family. A group of activists bought a page of advertising space in the paper to publicize a long list of instances where they claimed the Montgomery police had failed to investigate specific acts of violence against Dr King and his family. The full-page advertisement that appeared in the *New York Times* on 29 March 1960 was entitled 'Heed Their Rising Voices'.

Mr Sullivan, an elected public-affairs commissioner, sued because he considered the advertisement had impugned his reputation as a responsible official in Alabama. A jury in the Circuit Court of Montgomery County awarded him US$500,000 in damages, against the *New York Times* publication and four individual petitioners, African Americans (then referred to throughout the proceedings as 'Negros') and Alabama clergymen.

The Supreme Court stated that it could easily dispose of the argument 'that the constitutional guarantees of freedom of speech and of the press are inapplicable here, at least so far as the Times is concerned, because the allegedly libelous statements were published as part of a paid, "commercial" advertisement.' The judges argued that by allowing such an interpretation:

> The effect would be to shackle the First Amendment in its attempt to secure 'the widest possible dissemination of information from diverse and antagonistic sources' (*Associated Press* v. *United States*, 326 U.S. 1, 20). To avoid placing such a handicap upon the freedoms of expression, we hold that if the allegedly libelous statements would otherwise be constitutionally protected from the present judgment, they do not forfeit that protection because they were published in the form of a paid advertisement.
>
> [376 U.S. 254, 267]

The Supreme Court reversed the US$500,000 damages awarded at first instance in Alabama against the *New York Times* and four African-American ministers. This case established a First Amendment defence to defamation, effectively scaffolding freedom of speech by media in terms of a democratic discourse on behalf of US citizens. While not giving the media an unchecked right to publish criticism of public officials, it did offer media publishers, and specifically journalists, protection against defamation suits, even when some of the information published is incorrect or inaccurate. The judgment offered a wide shield for the media:

> Thus we consider this case against the background of a profound national commitment to the principle that debate on public issues

should be uninhibited, robust, and wide-open, and that it may well include vehement, caustic, and sometimes unpleasantly sharp attacks on government and public officials ... . We hold today that the Constitution delimits a State's power to award damages for libel in actions brought by public officials against critics of their official conduct.

[376 U.S. 254, 284]

From that time public officials, public figures and public-interest plaintiffs generally needed to provide evidence that media defendants published with knowledge of falsity or were motivated by actual malice. The burden of proof falls to the plaintiff. Subsequent important Supreme Court decisions shoring up defamation laws and available defences occurred in *Curtis Publishing Co* v. *Butts*, 1967, *Rosenbloom* v. *Metromedia*, 1971, *Gertz* v. *Welsh*, 1974, *Mary Alice Firestone* v. *Time Magazine*, 1976, and *Hustler Magazine* v. *Falwell*, 1988.

In the UK, unlike the US, there is no federal system or constitution, but there is a very long common-law heritage of defamation laws (or 'libel' as it is generally referred to in the UK). Landmark case law and key *stare decisis* cases include: *Ratcliffe* v. *Evans*, 1892, *Lewis* v. *Daily Telegraph*, 1964, *Reynolds* v. *Times Newspapers*, 1999, *Turkington* v. *Times*, 2000, *Jameel* v. *Wall Street Journal*, 2006. These cases have developed the full conceptual framework of defamation for issues ranging from the presumption of damage, public interest, truth, privilege and other defences, the 'reputations' of corporations, tests for what constitutes the meanings of defamation, questions of sexuality and reputation and categories of publication and damages. Libel laws are the only area of English law, civil or criminal, where the defendant is guilty until proven innocent. In other words, the burden of proof lies with the defendant to prove the substantive truth of the publication.

In the more recent cases, a public-interest defence has been created and refined, including notably by the *Reynolds* qualified privilege defence protecting responsible journalism. Although it is still not as broad as in the US, it has been noticeably influenced by developments in other jurisdictions, including the US and Australia (see for example, *Lange* v. *ABC* below). The case was brought by the former Irish Premier after the *Sunday Times* published material saying that he had lied to parliament and deceived his then coalition partner. In *Reynolds* the judiciary moved to create a public-interest defence, which was actually quite ineffectual at first, but it was then later bolstered into a workable defence in the *Jameel* case. *Reynolds* took the common law in new directions in shaping a public-interest defence; however, critics suggest that it did not chart the radically new course that is sometimes inferred. Robertson and Nicol describe the framework put in place by *Reynolds* to be generally considered by the media as a 'snare and an illusion' (2008, p. 98). It was a snare because it 'lured' editors and journalists into the witness box because they had failed to deliver on one or more of the ten requirements listed by Lord Nichols as necessary to constitute 'responsible journalism'; it was an illusion because the 'privilege' component of this qualified privilege defence has mostly been an impossibly high hurdle. Judges have been trained to accept such a privilege only in the most extreme instances of a moral or legal *duty* to publish, for example, in emergency circumstances such as food contamination. The ten 'pointers' of fair and responsible investigative journalism enumerated in *Reynolds* are in a sense the kind of journalism supported by the Press Complaints Commission Codes of ethical conduct in the UK, Australia's Press Council's Statement of Principles, or the Media Entertainment and Art Alliance's Code of Conduct. But the case was signposting a place for serious journalism in the public interest, capable of holding politicians to account or exposing other kinds of corruption or criminality.

This was the situation in the *Jameel* case, commenced in London by a wealthy Saudi businessman, which arose from imputations in a *Wall Street Journal* article, based on 'deep-throat' sources, that Mohammad Jameel had links to terrorism, and was being monitored by the Saudi government on behalf of the CIA. The jury awarded him personal damages of £30,000 and his company, £10,000. It cost the parties 'about £2 million' each (ibid., p. 161). Although clearly a loss for media freedom (the newspaper lost again in the Court of Appeal), the case elevated the possibility of 'serious', well-researched investigative journalism warranting a qualified-privilege defence. The first successful use of the *Reynolds/Jameel* defence was in *Chairman* v. *Orion Books*, 2007, when a policeman (in a lawsuit brought by the UK Police Federation) sued the publisher for imputations of corruption in BBC crime reporter Graham McLagan's book *Bent Coppers: The Inside Story of Scotland Yard's Battle against Police Corruption*. The defence had been denied by the trial judge but then permitted by the Court of Appeal, which was persuaded by McLagan's extensive research, thoroughness and honesty. The court ordered the plaintiff (Police Federation) to pay the full costs of the trial (ibid., p. xxiv).

Similarly, more recent changes in libel jurisprudence have arisen as a result of the influence of the European Convention for the Protection of Human Rights and Fundamental Freedoms, the Human Rights Act

1998 (UK), and case law flowing from the European Court of Human Rights. The Convention expressly recognizes the protections for reputation, or defamation laws, as a legitimate exception. Article 10 (1) provides that: 'Everyone has the right to freedom of expression. This right shall include freedom to hold opinions and to receive and impart information and ideas without interference by public authorities and regardless of frontiers.' Article 10 (2) refers to the necessary legal limits in the scope of these rights, including an exception '*for the protection of the reputation*' (Council of Europe, 2010, emphasis added).

At the same time, the courts of England and Wales have been required since 2000 to observe various conventions under sections 2 and 6 of the Human Rights Act, and to take into account (although they are not bound to follow) decisions in the European Court of Human Rights. This has meant that freedom of expression will be balanced against the right to privacy and, more consequentially, defamation law will become incorporated with privacy rights under the European Court of Human Rights' case law (Crook, 2010, p. 261). However, Robertson and Nicol are sceptical of some recent '7-Judge Eurocourt' interpretations of this 'balancing' act where free speech in Article 10 has become conflated with reputation and private life in Article 8, related to 'personal identity and psychological integrity' (2008, p. xxiii).

Crook has argued that there are advantages and disadvantages under both the US and UK common-law systems from a media publisher's perspective. While the culture to publish is freer in the US, in the less litigious UK 'people are more reluctant to take action because of cost, stress and the risk of enabling the repetition of the libel'. On the other hand, 'no win, no fee' opportunities as seen in 'conditional fee agreements' (CFAs) tend to democratize access for non-wealthy plaintiffs (Crook, 2010, p. 238). Yet the reality remains that libel laws are predominantly used by wealthy people who have the resources to gain access to the legal system. Legal aid has never been available for defamation suits in the UK (Jackson, 2009). Privilege defences in the UK tend to provide useful shields against defamatory content where this may also be for public-interest reasons. However, the prevalence of SLAPPS or 'strategic lawsuits against public participation', where corporations' use of deep-pocket financial resources, can be reasonably considered abuse of due process.

In Australia, defamation laws were substantially reformed in 2005/6, after several previous attempts had failed due to the difficulty involved when eight state and territory jurisdictions try to reach a consensus. From January 2006 uniform defamation laws took effect around

Australia: each state and territory introduced a Defamation Act, in very similar terms, enabling a nationally consistent approach to defamatory publications. However, these laws are basically derived from English common-law defamation, and there continues to be a significant amount of overlap between the two jurisdictions. Rolph *et al.* have made the point that inevitably, these divergent treatments of defamation, mixing common-law and statutory responses needed to be unified (2010, p. 207).

The objects of the unified legislation can be read as the policy priorities of the reformed defamation laws in Australia:

(a) to enact provisions to promote uniform laws of defamation in Australia;

(b) to ensure that the law of defamation does not place unreasonable limits on freedom of expression and, in particular, on the publication and discussion of matters of public interest and importance;

(c) to provide effective and fair remedies for persons whose reputations are harmed by the publication of defamatory matter;

(d) to promote speedy and non-litigious methods of resolving disputes about the publication of defamatory matter.

(Defamation Act, 2005, section 3)

Some of the changes followed those that were already present in other jurisdictions, for example, the limitation period for bringing defamation claims was in place in the UK. The key changes from previous laws relate to introducing standardized defences around Australia. Truth (or 'justification') is now a complete defence in New South Wales, Queensland and Tasmania (truth has always been a complete defence in Victoria, South Australia and Western Australia); apologies (or 'offers of amends') and innocent dissemination have been made statutory defences; and the category of qualified privilege for fair reports has been expanded. As mentioned above, potential monetary damages were capped at AUS$250,000 (indexed to the cost of living and judges may override this in certain situations and compensate for specific economic loss) and corporations can no longer sue for defamation, with the exception of organizations with fewer than ten employees.

In addition, the new laws have a provision to prevent 'forum shopping'; the reformed qualified-privilege defence includes the requirement that defendants need only prove the 'substantial truth' of the publication; they add a new statutory defence of 'fair and accurate' reports of court or parliamentary reports or a range of other 'public proceedings';

and a new statutory defence of qualified privilege based on the reasonableness of the publisher's conduct (echoing the UK common-law listed criteria in *Reynolds*, which requires responsible and ethical journalism). The uniform legislation, in keeping with the policy objective to ensure speedy and non-litigious methods of dispute resolution, introduces the 'offer of amends' mechanism (as mentioned, as a new defence) providing that, if and when an aggrieved individual accepts an offer of amends, that person may no longer pursue litigious claims in relation to that particular defamatory matter. In the event that a reasonable offer of amends is refused by an aggrieved person, the defendant may then use this refusal as a defence to the action.

The full benefits of these uniform law reforms, and whether a healthy balance has been struck between free communication and the protection of reputations, remain to be seen in the Australian context, although there is some evidence to suggest a reduction in the number of actions being pursued. In this regard, any curb on the 'libel tourism' problem that exists in the UK courts is undoubtedly a step in the right direction. In fact, there has been considerable criticism of the growth in practices of libel tourism in the UK, which are driven by the greater ease of suing successfully in England than in the US, and also the English courts' willingness to accept claims from litigants with limited connections to Britain. In the US, being a public figure means that the media have free rein to make criticisms, and if someone's reputation is genuinely tarnished, it's very difficult for that person to be compensated.

Media Practitioners and Defamation

To begin to get a sense of the legal implications of contemporary media practice, we can consider these different scenarios. Do you ever write for a university newspaper or a sports-club newsletter? Have you helped produce content for community television or radio? And to these more traditional activities we can now add various everyday new media practices:

- What messages do you post on blogs or send in multi-recipient emails?
- What content do you contribute to websites, including your Facebook profile?
- Do you have a Twitter account and tweet about events or people?
- Have you uploaded video to a video-sharing site like YouTube?

If you have created, used or distributed content in any of these ways, you would have been bound by the same legal principles as journalists and other media workers who write or produce content for metropolitan dailies, for radio or television, or 24/7 online. Everyone in the publishing industry has the same rights and obligations as other citizens. All are subject to the same laws. But the distinctive nature of media and journalistic work brings it into contact with specific areas of law every day. One of the key issues that can affect media practitioners in their everyday work concerns the laws of defamation.

It is not necessary to have a lawyer's knowledge, and defamation is certainly a very specialized area of the law, but media practitioners do need to recognize risky words and phrases; know when to seek legal advice in relation to controversial content; think about whether a publication is likely to land them in court; and make informed judgments about whether to proceed with a publication.

There are a variety of definitions of 'defamation' in common law and statutes. However a useful working definition is: 'The reduction of the reputation of another person in the minds of ordinary people, by exposing that person to ridicule, or by causing them to be shunned and avoided.'

Anyone may be defamed by what we call 'imputations', or the meanings between the lines. For example:

- suggestions of incompetence might offend a professional practitioner;
- suggestions of duplicity might offend someone who values the trust of the community, such as a youth worker or a real-estate agent;
- negative references to physical traits such as obesity might offend a sportsperson;
- suggestions of financial mismanagement might offend an accountant;
- stories of slovenly hygiene habits in the kitchen might offend a restaurateur;
- shocking party revelry might offend the kind of person who values their reputation as a role model for younger elite athletes; and
- a well-known media commentator tweeting a random, seemingly joky comment about the sexuality of a sports star may damage the person's reputation.

Although these examples may seem somewhat prosaic, they could lead to a successful claim through the courts for damage to reputation. The media have the potential to defame people every day. It is not only indirect imputations that you need to be aware of: direct statements, even if partially true, can trigger a defamation suit because the named person is prepared to contest the claim. Claiming the defamation to be unintentional cannot serve as a defence for media workers. Care and attention to detail is always necessary when a person's reputation is at stake. Nonetheless, it is only when someone has the will, the money and the knowledge of defamation laws to sue, that the publisher is held to account. Often, then, there is a 'chilling' effect on media work: the actual or perceived threat of possible legal action leads to self-censorship and tends to limit, or completely prevent, the publication of important public-interest material. As media-law academic Andrew Kenyon has argued: 'Media speech is chilled directly when lawyers recommend editing the content of publications, and is chilled structurally when journalists internalise the law's restrictive principles' (Dent and Kenyon, 2004; Kenyon, 2006).

Good Intentions

An action for defamation is usually a civil action defined in an Act of Parliament (although many jurisdictions also have criminal defamation, e.g. section 5 of the Libel Act, 1843 under English law), but inevitably an action will be influenced by the long and complex common-law history of defamation cases (Goldberg *et al.*, 2009, p. 377; Rolph *et al.*, 2010, p. 204).

In media workplaces, where the threat of defamation is constant, journalists often check only the articles they think might be defamatory, sometimes overlooking the very ones that turn out to be offensive. Just as ignorance is no excuse in criminal law, so the intentions of the writer or media publisher are usually irrelevant in a civil defamation action, and it will be insufficient to argue as a defence that you did not intend to defame someone. Equally, it will not be a defence that you did not intend the imputations, or meanings of your words.

The rules of defamation also apply irrespective of the means of distribution: you may be publishing in the traditional media to a multinational, national or local audience, 'micro-blogging' in 140 characters on Twitter, making an isolated comment on Facebook or emailing a small number of recipients. Media practitioners need to be aware that anyone involved in the publication may be liable: publishers, editors, journalists and their sources. Newspaper printers, distributors, newsagents/ retailers and internet-service providers can be sued, but they generally have a defence available known as 'innocent dissemination'.

A Question of Identity

Another pitfall for publishers can occur with mistaken identity. The claimant/plaintiff need not be the person the publisher/media practitioner intended to identify in the story; for an action to proceed, it is sufficient that the readers could presume the plaintiff was the person referred to in the article. Mistaken identity can occur with substitute or very similar names, identical names, group references, typing errors or omission of a name.

An article about an unnamed unscrupulous swimming-pool builder, in a particular suburb where there were three pool builders, could defame all three in that suburb, because readers could assume any one of them was the subject of the article. Conversely, an article containing a general statement about the untrustworthiness of television journalists would be safe, because no particular person would be identifiable in such a large field. Substitute names and absence of names are risky if the field is small enough for identification. Video footage or images that accompany reports can also imply unintended identity, as can textual inference: an apparently de-identified story may contain material that certain audiences will recognize as referencing a particular individual.

The Action

In commencing a defamation (or libel) case, the claimant or plaintiff (the person who sues) must first show that:

- the actual words used are defamatory;
- they refer to an identifiable person;
- they have been published;
- they could contribute to one or more of the following negative impacts:
  (a) exposure of the plaintiff to hatred, contempt, or ridicule, or
  (b) causing the plaintiff to be shunned and avoided by others, or
  (c) lowering the plaintiff in the estimation of ordinary, 'right-thinking' people.

(Goldberg *et al.*, 2009, p. 375)

Remember, to satisfy the requirements of 'publication' in a defamation action, a communication must reach at least one other person; hence, a fax, a postcard, an email, a comment on Facebook or a tweet may all be a publication.

So to have any chance of succeeding in an action the plaintiff must meet these prerequisites. To show loss of reputation, the plaintiff lists imputations. These are the messages that might result from the actual words – the meaning(s) or 'sting' readers might infer from the published material. Media practitioners can become adept at predicting imputations by adopting the 'walk in my shoes' approach. 'How would I feel if someone wrote this about me?' they might ask. 'How might another person interpret my words?' 'Could I defend in court the truth of these words and their intended or unintended meanings?' The priority of the media should be on publishing important public-interest material, and on legal advice, finding the right defences to fit the facts of your story in order that it may be published.

The Defence

If the plaintiff is successful in meeting the three elements of defamation, the case proceeds. As mentioned earlier, in jurisdictions other than the US, the burden of proof falls on the publisher, whose task it is to defend the words that have caused offence. It is, then, possible to 'defame' someone legally, if the publisher has a valid defence. In other words, the defendant needs to be able to produce evidence to prove their case.

Depending on the jurisdiction, the defences are either defined in statutes or available at common law, and the main ones are: truth (or 'justification'), privilege and opinion or comment. There are also other less frequently used defences: triviality, consent, innocent dissemination and offer of amends (in Australia's uniform laws). Which applies will depend on the circumstances. Practitioners must know and understand the main defences in order to make informed judgments about whether to publish or not.

Truth

Truth is often the first defence in a defamation action. In Australia or the UK, it is virtually impossible to defend words and imputations that are untrue. However, in the US, where the First Amendment gives greater legal protection to freedom of expression, it remains possible.

While Australian or British media practitioners have no equivalent protection for untrue publications, in the US the defence of truth can be affected by the constitutional guarantee of freedom of expression. This guarantee does not negate the need for truth and accuracy, either in the US, UK, Australia or in other jurisdictions; rather, it illustrates legal historical differences. The flipside is that, if you can prove truth, malice is irrelevant. In all free-speech countries, truth is crucial: no media outlet ought to be publishing unsubstantiated material, whether or not there is a constitutional freedom of expression.

The defence of truth ('justification') is not always as straightforward as it might seem. Imagine that two people meet in a dark city lane. One is a police officer, the other a shady underworld identity. The criminal hands a brown paper bag to the police officer. A crime journalist sees the exchange and writes in an article that the officer accepted a parcel from the other person in a city alley. The words are true – but the many meanings that spring from them might be untrue. The literal words imply a bribe.

If the publisher can show in court that the imputations are true, then those imputations set or confirm the level of the reputation of the plaintiff; hence, defamation would be impossible since a viewer, reader or listener is unable to think less of that person. A plaintiff usually lists several imputations, and if the defendant fails to prove just one of them, the defence of truth will fail. In one of the most famous contemporary libel cases fast-food chain McDonald's sued campaigners Helen Steel and David Morris, a gardener and a postman, over the distribution of a leaflet: *What's Wrong with McDonald's?*. In *McDonald's Corp* v. *Steel and Anor*, the so-called 'McLibel Trial', the court found the pair had defamed McDonald's (Goldberg *et al.*, 2009, p. 403). The defendants' leaflet conveyed a number of imputations including that eating McDonald's fast food had serious health implications. The trial was the longest-running trial in English legal history, extending over two and a half years. The single judge presiding over the trial, Justice Bell, handed down his judgment in 1997. Having proved the truth of some of the imputations, e.g. McDonald's 'exploits' children and disseminated generally misleading advertising, the defendants were unable to prove the others and ordered to pay damages of £60,000.

Subsequently, in 1999, the Court of Appeal ruled that it was fair comment to say that McDonald's employees worldwide 'do badly in terms of pay and conditions', and that 'if one eats enough McDonald's food, one's diet may well become high in fat, with a real risk of heart disease', reducing the damages to £20,000 (Crook, 2010, p. 245). The

'McLibel' case had two important outcomes: it put the public spotlight on the abuse of defamation laws against individuals lacking the necessary resources, and it kick-started a much bigger PR campaign against the fast-food giant, including the well-known 2004 documentary by independent filmmaker Morgan Spurlock, *Supersize Me*. But Steel and Morris didn't stop there. They took the British government to the European Court of Human Rights in Strasbourg, arguing that UK defamation laws were oppressive and unfair, and that they had been denied a fair trial in the UK. The court upheld their claims, finding that their rights to free expression under Article 10 of the European Convention, and to a fair trial, had been breached (ibid.).

An interesting feature of Australia's now uniform defamation laws is that corporations with more than ten employees are not able to sue (Defamation Act NSW, 2005, section 9). The underlying policy intent of legislators is concerned with redressing inequality in access to these laws, including the asymmetrical power of corporations: simply the idea of *corporations* having 'a reputation'. Clearly this has ruled out the possibility of a McLibel-style case even starting in Australia post-2006.

So, in order to mount a successful defence of truth, defendants need to prove that all the alleged defamatory imputations in the 'matter complained of' were 'substantially true'. This can be a very difficult task: defendants may be able to establish the truth of an imputation, but to prove the facts upon which the imputation is based can be much more difficult.

Privilege

Defamation law recognizes that on certain 'privileged occasions' the public interest in people speaking out will outweigh an individual's right to protect their reputation. There is an absolute privilege to publish otherwise defamatory material in reports of open sessions in parliaments and the courts. Accordingly, the publication of defamatory material from such proceedings will be completely immune from the laws of defamation, even if it is couched in the most scurrilous terms. The defence of 'absolute privilege' means complete immunity from the laws of defamation based on the principle of 'open justice' that allows the courts and the parliaments to function in a fearlessly independent manner.

A second form of privilege arises in circumstances of qualified privilege. This allows the defence to be available provided certain specific conditions are met. The defence of 'qualified privilege' refers to content or statements that might otherwise be regarded as defamatory, but which are protected from prosecution. The defence of qualified privilege is dependent upon complete accuracy in the media report in question.

Discussion of political and government matters, referred to as 'political qualified privilege', is protected in most common-law jurisdictions and treated as a defence in its own right in Australia. This defence has a special significance in Australian jurisprudence, having its genesis in a series of free-speech cases in the early 1990s, including the *Lange* case (in which a former prime minister of New Zealand sued the Australian Broadcasting Corporation for defamation over imputations in an investigative television programme). In that case, the High Court held that the constitution created an 'implied guarantee' of a freedom to communicate on political and government matters. The defence is sometimes called the 'Lange defence': *Lange* v. *Australian Broadcasting Corporation* [1997] 189 CLR 520; online at www.austlii.edu.au.

Opinion and Comment

The publication of opinion and comment is protected from a defamation action provided that certain conditions exist. Essentially, this defence enables the free expression of opinions and comments and can apply to commentary, analysis, reviews, satire and cartoons. The defence protects an honestly held opinion, however extreme or unreasonable it seems. The honest-opinion defence (in Australia the statutory defence is similar to the common-law defence of 'fair comment') applies to material presented as opinion, not fact. For example, a restaurant review which baldly stated 'The lobster was tough and overcooked' is presented as fact. The fair-comment defence would therefore be unlikely to hold. But if the journalist had written, 'In my opinion, on that occasion it seemed to me that the lobster was tough and overcooked', the fair-comment defence may apply, if the statement were the genuinely held opinion of the reviewer journalist, properly researched and without malice. Robertson and Nicol note that the opinion must have a factual basis:

> The defence of fair comment will not succeed if the comment is made without any factual basis. An opinion cannot be conjured out of thin air – it must be based on something. And that something should either be accurately stated in the article or at least referred to

with sufficient clarity to enable the reader to identify it. It is not necessary to set out all the evidence for the writer's opinion: a summary of it or a reference to where it can be found is sufficient. Even a passing reference is sufficient if readers will understand what is meant.

(2008, p. 153)

The honest-opinion defence is particularly useful for restaurant reviewers, music and theatre critics and editorial writers, but it can apply to anyone expressing a view publicly. By definition, opinion and comment need not be provable, just fairly based and without malice. It should be noted that 'malice' is a technical legal term that tends to be defined very broadly.

Defamation on the Internet

In the events leading to the landmark Dow Jones case (*Dow Jones & Company Inc* v. *Gutnick* [2002] 210 CLR 575), defamatory material published in the US was downloaded in the Australian state of Victoria, where the reputation and identity of the plaintiff, businessman Joseph Gutnick, was well known.

In this landmark case the defendant, Dow Jones, operated an online news subscription service 'Barons'. The content was uploaded to servers in New Jersey in the US. The plaintiff, Joseph Gutnick, a Melbourne investment and share-trading businessman, having downloaded the content in Victoria, claimed certain material to be defamatory. Basically, the imputations were that Gutnick had connections to a convicted money launderer and fraudster.

The plaintiff commenced proceedings in the Supreme Court of Victoria, in Australia. The defendant meanwhile sought to have the action struck out on the grounds that Australian law should, like the libel laws applying in the US, recognize that in the case of the internet, publication occurred when the subscription magazine content was uploaded in New Jersey. They also argued, unsuccessfully, that the case should be heard in the US under US law. As discussed earlier, defamation laws in the US tend to be more favourable to defendants (publishers) than in other common-law countries. The plaintiff's legal team successfully argued that Victoria was the most appropriate place to bring the action, since Gutnick lived in Victoria, and that was where he was most likely to suffer the greatest harm to his reputation.

The High Court established that the action could proceed in Victoria, despite the fact that the material was written, produced and published on a US website. In a unanimous judgment in Mr Gutnick's favour, the High Court held that the general rule was that defamation occurs at the place where the material is made available in a comprehensive form: *Dow Jones & Company Inc* v. *Gutnick* (online at www.austlii.edu.au). In the case of the internet, this occurs when material is downloaded and read via a browser; and it is the place where the content is downloaded that any damage to reputation may occur. The action was therefore validly commenced in Victoria, and the High Court found that Mr Gutnick had indeed been defamed, awarding him significant damages, and ordered that the plaintiffs pay his legal costs.

But the wider significance of the Dow Jones case is that it illustrates how the internet problematizes the issue of jurisdiction. That is, since defamation laws have evolved in specific geographic jurisdictions, the internet – which crosses all boundaries – now complicates the notion of 'publication' as it had previously applied to media outlets. It cannot be assumed that statements can be made safely online just because they relate to individuals in another country, or because someone has already said it on a website.

The identity of the publisher and disseminator of the material is critical. The internet-service provider cannot be expected to check all content in the same way that traditional media can check content prior to broadcast or print publication. Hence the ISP, and in some cases also a website, might have the defence of innocent dissemination (just as a newspaper seller may have such a defence in relation to a traditional newspaper story).

The second consideration is the place of publication and location of the audience. The location of the ISP, the location of the sender (or 'uploader') of the material and the location of the audience may all be anywhere in world.

The Dow Jones case means that any person in the world who places content on the web that could be viewed in a country where a plaintiff is identified, does so not only subject to the local laws of the jurisdiction where they happen to be, but also subject to the potentially different laws of the country where the person is identified. And, in reverse, material uploaded in a particular country may fall foul of laws in other places where content is downloaded. This will be particularly significant where the foreign laws are more advantageous to a plaintiff identified in the publication than local defamation laws. These questions now have to be considered in relation to the place where the plaintiff's reputation is most at stake.

Legislation in the US and the UK has attempted to define the separation between internet provider and publisher, thus creating a demarcation to protect the ISP from liability. However, the near ubiquity of the internet suggests that there could be significant global (i.e. financial) defamation fallout for the fastest-growing medium. Although the case specifically concerns defamation laws, *Dow Jones & Company Inc* v. *Gutnick* has wider implications for internet law and governance in general because it has established the importance of a distinction between origination of content (uploading) and the point of consumption (downloading). In effect, the case means that a person or media organization making material available online could potentially be sued in just about any jurisdiction where a media platform can be accessed and proceedings can be commenced. However, in practice, as we have seen, there are many other complex jurisdictional issues that may bear on this process (sometimes called 'conflict of laws' principles), including how the specific laws are interpreted judicially, in addition to how their enforcement operates internationally (Goldsmith and Wu, 2008).

Defamation and Ethical Risks in the Use of Social Networking

For further evidence of the continuing use of defamation laws to redress perceived harm to reputation by media industries, we can look to the growing number of actions brought by plaintiffs over libel comments arising on new social-media platforms.

The proliferation of defamatory incidents in social media, including Facebook and Twitter, indicates that defamation can occur no matter which medium conveys the content that impacts on an individual's reputation. Since the fundamental rule in media defamation is that, if content contains defamatory material harmful to a person's reputation, identifies a person and is published (communicated to at least one other person), it can be considered defamation under common law (Goldberg *et al.*, 2009, p. 375). This means that a comment on Twitter may give rise to a defamation action, even if a person had only a single follower other than the plaintiff.

Recent controversies can be used to illustrate some social-networking hotspots. For example, an incident involving Julie Posetti, a former journalist and now academic, and her Twitter comments about editorial practices at News Corporation, led to the *Australian* editor-in-chief Chris Mitchell launching a defamation action. This incident showed the ease with which the elements of defamation may arise from the use of the Twitter platform. The comments tweeted by Posetti were sufficient to cast negative aspersions about Mitchell's professional editorial style, and contained the imputations that he was an overly interventionist editor. Posetti's tweet quoted the *Australian*'s former rural reporter Asa Wahlquist as allegedly saying 'in the lead up to the election the Ed-in-Chief was increasingly telling me what to write'. Other comments quoted Wahlquist as saying that writing on climate change for the *Australian* was 'absolutely excruciating. It was torture.' Hardly scathing personal indictments, you would think, and yet enough for Mitchell to feel that his reputation had been impugned (Elliott, 2010).

A number of successful Twitter defamation actions have been brought in the UK and the US. In the UK, it was reported that the first successful Twitter defamation case occurred when local council politician and former Mayor of Caerphilly in Wales, Colin Elsbury, agreed to pay £3,000 ($US4,825) in damages and to publish an apology on Twitter to his political rival Eddie Talbot. Elsbury was also required to pay Talbot's legal fees, estimated at £50,000 (Clickdocs, 2011). Talbot sued Elsbury after the latter had claimed in a June 2009 tweet that Talbot had been 'forcibly removed' from a polling station by police during a local election in Wales. Elsbury later admitted it had been a case of mistaken identity, but had then failed to correct the first tweet. Talbot was seeking election to the local council, but Elsbury actually won. Again, to an outsider looking at the rough and tumble of political media reporting, this is hardly a major character assassination. Yet Talbot's lawyer successfully argued in the High Court in Wales that the tweet was untrue and defamatory, and left his client open to ridicule (Associated Press, 2011).

But undoubtedly the Twitter case receiving the most publicity to date has involved the frontwoman of the US rock band Hole, Courtney Love, who was sued by Los Angeles fashioner designer Dawn Simorangkir after she allegedly publicly attacked and defamed her in a series of tweets (and in posts on her MySpace and Etsy accounts) in March 2009 (Perpetua, 2011a, 2011b). It was reported that a dispute between Love and Simorangkir started when the fashion designer sought to charge Love very inflated prices for her trend-setting clothing. Love then allegedly attacked Simorangkir for capitalizing on her fame, tweeting that she was a 'drug-pushing prostitute' with a history of assault, and who had lost custody of her child. Originally set down for trial, the parties negotiated and settled out of court with Love paying Simorangkir $US430,000 in damages (ibid.).

Had the matter proceeded to court, apparently Simorangkir's legal team would have argued that Love's false statements in effect destroyed their client's fashion career, and this entitled the designer to large sums of monetary compensation in damages, for income foregone (Reuters, 2011).

Increasingly, as influential celebrities have vast numbers of followers on social-media platforms, the Love case raises both legal and ethical questions regarding whether celebrities, like the news media and promotion media, should be liable for the consequences if they intentionally put around untrue and damaging statements to their loyal readers. In social media the misuse of celebrity power becomes a question of the power of celebrity agency, rather than the role of an editor or production team, as it would be in the context of a traditional media story (Turner *et al.*, 2000).

Above all, these cases indicate to users of social media that, despite the ease and informal style of Twitter, Facebook and their ilk, the usual rules of defamation clearly apply to these new media platforms. With the rising popularity of social-media platforms, the question of how journalists are now using social media in their practices has been looming on the media-practice ethics radar for several years. The 2010/11 edition of the Media, Entertainment and Art Alliance's *Life in the Clickstream* Report notes, 'social media tools such as Facebook and Twitter are gaining increasing acceptance as ways to source stories (44 per cent) and to reach new audiences (52 per cent)' (MEAA, 2010, p. 22).

It can be seen that various practices involving social-media platforms all require that ethical judgments be exercised in varying degrees. Online journalistic practices include the use of social media to:

- source news stories;
- channel personal communication;
- engage with readers directly – giving a more personal face to a media outlet;
- engage in conversations with audiences in relation to an editorial;
- express personal views and opinions.

From the reporting of natural disasters such as floods in Australia to the Japan earthquake, to major news events like democracy movements in the Middle East and North Africa, it is clear that social-media networking sites allow the most powerful images sent by witnesses to live events to be transmitted online, well before they reach television screens or mainstream news organizations.

The Twitter hashtag sign is used to search for relevant information for media events. For example, in the Queensland flooding in Australia, the hashtag '#Qld' (an abbreviation for the state of 'Queensland') became a way to elicit news about the unfolding damage wrought by rising floodwaters. In early stages of reporting the 2011 earthquake in Japan, YouTube was one of the most popular ways to actually source news. Indeed in many of these kinds of situations social media are the *only* way to source breaking news. Questions of news values and veracity inevitably require ethical decision-making and judgment.

Journalists often include their employer's name in their Twitter biography, with some using standard disclaimers, and others more casual disclaimers to indicate that the account is a personal one. There are important ethical and legal consequences in these trends. First, this tends to indicate that the opinions espoused are those of the individual, despite the fact that their employer can still be easily identified as associated with the individual. Second, naming an employer could also give rise to questions regarding the ability of the person to objectively report the facts of a story when strong opinions have been expressed via a personal account.

Because news organizations are concerned about being brought into disrepute by employees' use of social media, and being held accountable for defamation, and in certain cases have cautioned, disciplined and stood down staff members over their personal online comments, this has led some organizations to develop social-media policies. News organizations are seeing direct benefits from providing staff with adequate guidelines and training on the appropriate use of social media (Sankey, 2010).

Research by the Pew Research Centre's 'Project for Excellence in Journalism' indicates that news stories reported on different social-media platforms have their own dynamic and relationship to mainstream news-reporting agendas. The researchers found that: Twitter was even less likely to share the traditional media agenda; and, stories that gain traction in social media do so quickly, often within hours of initial reports, and leave quickly as well – just 5 per cent of the top five stories on Twitter remained among the top stories the following week; but, in the mainstream press, on the other hand, fully 50 per cent of the top five stories one week remained a top story a week later; social-media players espouse a different agenda than the mainstream media – blogs still rely heavily on the traditional press – and primarily just a few outlets within that – for their information. More than 99 per cent of the stories linked to in blogs came from legacy outlets such as newspapers and broadcast networks (Pew Research Centre, 2010).

It is precisely the examination of this relationship to the mainstream (or traditional) media that can assist us in teasing out the ethical and legal hotspots. The inherent platform differences (affordances, constraints, news agendas) between these media can shine a light on where potential problems may exist. Unless there is a focused effort by media professionals to bring ethical and legal principles to the fore in their use of social media, any number of issues may be triggered.

The perils involved when journalists resort to Facebook pages as a source for news stories constitute a frequently heard tale. The Australian Broadcasting Corporation's weekly *Media Watch* television programme, which has shone a spotlight on many unethical media practices, has often pointed to incidents involving Facebook and social media in general. An incident involving the Queensland regional newspaper, the *Warwick Daily News*, was an example of a sensational news story that went off the rails, particularly from the editor's perspective. In 2010 the paper ran a front-page story headlined 'These Women Teach Your Children', which began 'two female Warwick State High School ... teachers are being investigated after a series of raunchy photos were broadcast across social networking website Facebook'. *Media Watch* exposed the way in which the photos were obtained, and the broader context of the teachers' photos (ABC, 2010). The images accompanying the story show the two teachers in sexy poses in a bathroom in faux school uniforms with fishnet stockings. The images, while 'suggestive', were hardly pornographic. *Media Watch* reported that one of the journalists was a Facebook 'friend' of one of the teachers and was thus alerted to the existence of the images and comments. The Australian MEAA Code of Ethics has a provision urging journalists to respect privacy in balance with the public interest, and the Press Council's Statement of Principles contains a similar clause. (This is discussed further in the next chapter.) On one level this is a fairly low-key local news story exploiting schoolteachers' private social lives. However, on another level, in a small country town, the damage inflicted to people's reputations can be highly consequential. Not surprisingly, the two teachers sued the newspaper for defamation.

The formats and presentation of online news stories are in themselves potentially an important element for ethical consideration: it is standard practice for news sites to include 'participatory' processes, and the ability to 'talk back' can be seen historically as an evolving component from traditional media formats. Richard Collins's argument in relation to trust in online news media raises key ethical consequences, particularly given the near ubiquity of feedback or 'have your say' mechanisms in news media formats. This is not just a feature of celebrity commentators: standard news-online news formats often include 'comment' boxes. As Collins argues:

> The dialogic potentiality of Web 2.0 media may mitigate, if not solve, some of the problems of trust that beset 'one to many' mass media. To make such a claim may seem unusual in the context of the general emphasis of Internet studies which predominantly addresses the perceived problems and damaging potentiality of the media and the Internet in particular. There can be no doubt that there are significant negative issues to be addressed: fraud, spam, phishing, and the dissemination of potentially harmful and/or offensive material … but attention to these has masked general recognition of the positive potential of the Internet and the trust-enhancing capabilities of networked online collaboration.
>
> (2009, p. 72)

Whether mainstream online news media, that is branded mastheads, can be characterized as the 'fifth estate' or as representing a 'new form of accountability', as some commentators have argued, is at best a moot point. The ability to express an opinion or otherwise react to a news item does not amount to equal editorial authority in correcting inaccurate or misinformed content. It is often simply the opportunity to put an alternative interpretation of events. If a reader is so motivated to correct an inaccurate, unfair or misleading report, the principal existing procedural method to do so remains the lodging of a complaint with the relevant media regulatory body.

Recent research titled 'Australian Media's Use of Facebook Postings to Report Events of National Interest' explores how Australian newspapers used the social-networking site Facebook in reporting three different news events: the disappearance of Australian backpacker Britt Lapthorne; the death of four-year-old Darcey Freeman; and the devastating 'Black Saturday' Victorian bushfires (Dickens *et al.*, 2010).

The research identifies the main ways in which information from Facebook was utilized by journalists within these news stories, which may all give rise to certain risks in terms of accuracy, fairness, privacy and reputation. Their specific findings included:

- Social-networking sites provide journalists with access to material that may be difficult to obtain through other means and that can variously assist them in producing their stories.

- The rise of social networking presents new challenges for journalists in relation to how they use information ethically and responsibly, and the privacy implications associated with media reporting of postings on social-networking sites.
- Facebook supplies journalists with readily accessible content that can provide the primary source for news stories, or supplementary information through which they can emphasize particular aspects of a news story (ibid.).

Quotes from the newsworthy individuals on their Facebook pages were most often employed to create an insight into a particular personality. The authors found that journalists use Facebook as a 'virtual background tool' to investigate and create a character profile of persons involved in the news stories they are covering. The significance of privacy is a key theme in the research. The authors note:

> Facebook contains over 40 pieces of recognisably personal information ranging from sexual preference, relationship status and offline contact information. There is conflicting information about whether members of the public understand the privacy limitations of social networking sites such as Facebook, and the expectations members of the public have about online privacy.

It can be seen that, with the rise of social media, questions concerning the use of confidential information and privacy have become even more pressing than they have been when in the hands of traditional media practitioners. In the following chapter we turn to legal and ethical issues that arise in both traditional and new media contexts, as a result of misuses of confidential personal information and privacy conditions.

References

Associated Press (2011) 'Damages Being Paid in UK Twitter Defamation Case', ABCNews.co/AP, 12 March, available at http://abcnews.go.com/Technology/wireStory?id=13123027.
Australian Broadcasting Corporation (2010) Media Watch 'A Lesson in Facebook Friends', Episode 11, 19 April, available at http://www.abc.net.au/tv/mediawatch.
BBC (2008) 'Papers Paying Damages to the McCanns', BBC News, available at http://news.bbc.co.uk/2/hi/uk_news/7303801.stm.

Belnaves, M., S. Donald and B. Shoesmith (2009) *Media Theories and Approaches: A Global Perspective* (Basingstoke: Palgrave Macmillan).

Clickdocs (2011) 'Politician Loses "Twibel" Case', 18 March, available online at http://www.clickdocs.co.uk/news/view.asp?ID=1252.

Collins, R. (2009) 'Trust and Trustworthiness in the Fourth and Fifth Estates', *International Journal of Communication* vol. 2.

Council of Europe (2010) *Convention for the Protection of Human Rights and Fundamental Freedoms as Amended by Protocols No. 11 and No. 14*, Rome, 4.XI.1950, available online at http://conventions.coe.int/treaty/en/treaties/html/005.htm.

Crook, T. (2010) *Comparative Media Law and Ethics* (London and New York: Routledge).

Defamation Act (2005) NSW, available online at http://portsea.austlii.edu.au/cgi-pit/renderFrag.py?frag=/home/www/pit/xml/nsw/act/450fc6ebb32220f4.xml&date=20101123.

Dent, C. and A. Kenyon (2004) 'Defamation Law's Chilling Effect: A Comparative Content Analysis of Australian and US Newspapers', *Media & Arts Law Review* vol. 9 no. 2, pp. 89–111.

Dickens, M., S. Thomas and K. Holland (2010) *Proceedings of the 2010 Communications Policy Research Forum* (Sydney: Network Insight).

Elliott, G. (2010) 'The *Australian*'s Chris Mitchell to Sue Julie Posetti for Defamation', *Australian*, 26 November, available online at News.com.au.

Gibb, F. (2009) 'It's Official: London Is Libel Capital of the World', *Times Online*, 24 November.

Goldberg. D., G. Sutter and I. Walden *et al.* (2009) *Media Law and Practice* (Oxford: Oxford University Press).

Goldsmith, J. and T. Wu (2008) *Who Controls the Internet? Illusions of a Borderless World*, 2nd edn (New York: Oxford University Press).

Henderson, M. (2009) 'Cardiologist Will Fight Libel Case "to Defend Free Speech"', *Times Online*, Business Law, 26 November.

Henderson, M. (2010) 'Science Writer Simon Singh Wins Bitter Libel Battle', *Times Online*, 15 April.

Jackson, R. (2009) Lord Justice, Court of Appeals Judge, Transcript, Sir Rupert Jackson, House of Commons Minutes of Evidence Taken before the Culture, Media and Sport Committee Enquiry into Press Standards, Privacy and Libel, UK Parliament, *Hansard*, 19 May.

Kenyon, A. T. (2006) *Defamation: Comparative Law and Practice* (London: UCL Press).

MEAA (2010) *Life in the Clickstream*, in a discussion of the findings of the 'The Future of Quality Journalism' project.

Monbiot, G. (2008) 'How Can the Rich Still Be Buying Our Silence with This 13th-century Law?' *Guardian.co.uk*, 17 September, available online at http://www.guardian.co.uk/commentisfree/2008/sep/17/matthiasrath.medialaw.

Perpetua, M. (2011a) 'Courtney Love Sued for Twitter Defamation', *Rolling Stone*, 5 January.

Perpetua, M. (2011b) 'Courtney Love Settles Twitter Defamation Suit for $430,000', 3 March.

Pew Research Centre (2010) *Project for Excellence in Journalism*, 'New Media, Old Media: How Blogs and Social Media Agendas Relate and Differ from Traditional Press', 23 May, available online at http://www.journalism.org/analysis_report/blogosphere.

Reuters (2011) 'Courtney Love's Tweets Lead to Court Trial', 5 January, available online at *Reuters.com*.

Robertson, G. and A. Nicol (2008) *Media Law*, 5th edn (London: Penguin).

Rolph, D., M. Vitins and J. Bannister (2010) *Media Law. Cases, Materials and Commentary* (Melbourne: Oxford University Press).

Sankey, D. (2010) Personal interview transcription. 3 September.

Turner, G., F. Bonner and P. D. Marshall (2000) *Fame Games: The Production of Celebrity in Australia* (Cambridge: Cambridge University Press).

US Supreme Court, *New York Times Co.* v. *Sullivan* 376 U.S. 254 (1964), Certiorari to the Supreme Court of Alabama, no. 39, Findlaw, available online at http://caselaw.lp.findlaw.com/scripts/getcase.pl?navby=case&court=us&vol=376&page=254#t3.

4 Confidential Information and Privacy

In May 2010, the transport minister David Campbell in the embattled New South Wales Labour government led by then Premier Kristina Keneally, announced he had resigned as a minister. His resignation came shortly before an evening news bulletin on the commercial, free-to-air television channel outed the minister as leading a 'double life' as a gay man for twenty-five years. The report included low-quality vision, taken by private investigators and acquired by the Seven Network, of Campbell leaving a gay sauna club, 'Ken's of Kensington', in darkness. The incident quickly became a *cause célèbre* for privacy and gay-rights advocates: it served to highlight that Australia has no general tort for breach of privacy at common law or in a statute, unlike the more robust frameworks that exist in other comparable democracies; and it also pointed to shortcomings in the rather flimsy protections offered under the commercial TV industry's code of practice, supervised by the media regulator, the Australian Communications and Media Authority (ACMA). Media commentators noted that this was an attack on the private life of a gay man, and had nothing to do with journalism 'in the public interest'.

Subsequently complaints were lodged (not by Campbell) with the ACMA, which was required to adjudicate it since the complainants were dissatisfied with the first-instance responses they had received from the broadcaster. The broadcaster's submission argued that privacy guidelines accompanying the commercial television code of practice envisage a range of circumstances justifying media intrusion into an individual's privacy including 'matters of politics, government and public administration'. Those circumstances echo the public-interest 'privilege' defences discussed in the previous chapter. Seven defended their report using a number of public-interest-styled defences based on the minister's actions: the act of his resignation; the use of public resources including driving a tax-payer-funded car to the club; the minister's handling of recent issues within his portfolio; the hypocrisy of the minister portraying himself as a family man in Christmas cards sent to people in his electorate; the requirement that the minister conform to the standards of propriety and discretion; and that, as a former police minister, he could have left himself open to blackmail. The ACMA weighed the merits of these defences (and related actions) and found only one to be persuasive: the minister's resignation itself. Clearly this meant that all the other defences were only assertions that the broadcaster used to justify what the majority of journalistic commentary saw as a blatant breach of an individual's privacy. The ACMA's investigation report into the code-of-practice breaches was silent on the implied scenario of there being no available public-interest defence had Campbell not resigned as a member of parliament (ACMA, 2010). Arguably the journalist in this case had acted unethically in assembling a patchwork of assertions and smears for a media scalp. Yet the regulator found that there had been no breach of the relevant privacy code. The ethical philosophy frameworks discussed in Chapter 1 alert us to many of the dilemmas for media practice implicated in this kind of media storm: virtue ethics and character, a golden mean for actions (Aristotelian); duty to report fairly and honestly, treating media subjects with humanity as ends, and not as merely a means to a story (Kantian); the need to avoid harm (Confucian, Buddhist); and maximizing 'happiness' for a majority (Utilitarian).

In this chapter we consider the breaches of privacy or data-protection laws and codes of practice that are frequently perpetrated by media practitioners. We ask critical-practice questions such as: Do you use recorded images or sound without people's express consent? Are there particular media scenarios where a right to privacy might be reasonably expected? What are the limits of permissible information gathering by the media? A succession of cases in the UK have upheld that the right to privacy should be reasonably expected including in *Campbell* v. *Mirror Group Newspapers Ltd* (2003), *Douglas and Ors v. Hello! Ltd* (2005), *Murray* v. *Big Pictures (UK)* (2008); and, under European Union law and Article 8 of the European Convention of Human Rights, *Von Hannover* v. *Germany* (2005). As mentioned in Chapter 3, following the introduction of the Human Rights Act 1998, the law of breach of confidence has in effect been 'shoehorned' to encompass a cause of action for misuse of private information. In addition to these key cases we will also consider the origins of the term 'privacy' and its dispersal across various categories of law; briefly review related laws including information privacy and confidentiality, consider hotspots such as CCTV and issues arising from online media platforms including Facebook; and conclude with a discussion of ethical philosophy and privacy.

As noted in the previous chapter, privacy is an area of law that may, in certain situations, cross over with questions of defamation and confidentiality, blurring neat demarcations between rights, responsible media performance and legal redress. We live in times of shifting relations between the public and private spheres. Media and communications are actively involved in this process of redefining social and cultural understandings of the values we refer to as 'privacy'. Think of the way we now communicate in public spaces. When we travel on public transport, we use mobile and online communication devices to have, on occasions, fairly intimate conversations with those we care about, or other conversations that could be defined as 'private'. Or, to take another example from the mediated public sphere, think of 'reality'-television formats. Contestants (and it usually is some kind of 'contest') are a weird mix of celebrity and 'ordinary', and audiences can engage with a hybridity of personal, private and yet at the same time highly public human interactions. Social-networking sites like Facebook and other kinds of 'mass self communication', as Castells (2007) has described it, also have these hybrid private and public elements. In fact, the software usually allows people to have a graduated private/public 'switch' on their personal profiles, capable of recognizing social distinctions between family and friends who are in a closer network, and all the others whom they permit to become part of the wider network of generic 'friends'. Commercially driven experiments with personal privacy have attracted public resistance and official scrutiny. The Federal Trade Commission (FTC) and congressional privacy committee members in the US have investigated the way third-party applications gather and transmit personally identifiable information about Facebook users and those users' friends (FTC, 2010). The introduction of federal and state level 'do not track' laws and regulations, backed up with FTC enforcement powers, is evidence of the seriousness that these developments now pose. They provide for an opt-out for consumers to protect privacy and prevent data collection by advertisers and other third parties from social-networking sites (Goodin, 2011).

In these developments we can see that the line between the public and private sphere is constantly being redrawn. So it should be becoming clearer that 'privacy is essentially normative and, as such, the idea of the private changes over time, with part of that change being driven by technological change affecting communications' (Morrison *et al.*, 2007, p. 199). The Australian Law Reform Commission (ALRC) in its 2008 report notes:

It does appear that young people are more comfortable than their parents, and certainly their grandparents, in sharing personal information, photos and other material on social networking websites. The question is whether this represents the beginnings of an enduring cultural shift, or simply the eternal recklessness of youth, played out in a new medium and utilising new technology. Put another way, will today's teenagers be horrified in a decade's time when prospective employers – and prospective partners and in-laws – can easily 'google up' intimate and potentially embarrassing images and information?

Through Article 8 of the European Convention of Human Rights and the Human Rights Act 1998 (UK) a right to privacy is now enshrined in UK common law; and in the US, the right to privacy has the most highly developed jurisprudence of Anglophone common-law countries (based on a *Harvard Law Review* article entitled 'The Right to Privacy' in 1890 by Warren and Brandeis), giving litigants an alternative to defamation laws, which are much weaker. Privacy as a human right is enshrined in several international instruments: in particular, the International Covenant on Civil and Political Rights (1966) and the Universal Declaration on Human Rights (1948). The language of rights is again being used, but this time for cyberspace. The Commercial Privacy Bill of Rights Act 2011 was introduced into the US Congress by Senators Kerry and McCain, and was hotly contested by those corporations who have the most to lose. It would require 'companies trading online to provide clear notice about what information is being collected and for what purposes' (Clark, 2011).

Origins of Privacy

While a respected value for several hundred years, 'modern obsessions with privacy are largely rooted in the twentieth century, particularly the years following the Second World War'. As Kenyon and Richardson argue, the precise reasons for invoking notions of privacy vary with the context and change over time (2006).

European civilian lawyers will reference the European Convention on Human Rights, with its important provisions for security of private life together with the protection of freedom of expression, arising from the war years. American lawyers would certainly refer to the seminal writings of Samuel D. Warren and Louis D. Brandeis, where 'privacy' is defined as 'The state or condition of being alone, undisturbed, or free from public attention, as a matter of choice or right.' Their work preceded the twentieth century by only a single decade and yet was remarkably prescient for the way processes of mediatization would, from that time, shape how people conceived their social lives. It was the start of a long chain of US common-law cases recognizing a right to privacy.

English lawyers may note that privacy stems from its common-law beginnings in the landmark constitutional case of *Entick* v. *Carrington* in the eighteenth century, 'but sometimes find it difficult to explain emerging concerns about privacy except as a European phenomenon swept to England under the impetus of the European Convention' (ibid., p. 2).

In fact, a matrix of factors in technologies, media and culture and in models of regulation, have accelerated demands for privacy protection in many media systems. The wedding of Hollywood stars, Michael Douglas and Catherine Zeta-Jones in 2000 offers some insight into the UK's celebrity-obsessed tabloid media (*Douglas and Ors* v. *Hello! Ltd*). A media debate over privacy, confidentiality and defamation was sparked when the magazines *Hello!* and *OK!* published photographs taken at the wedding. *OK!* paid for exclusive rights to publish the Douglas–Zeta-Jones wedding photos, while *Hello!* published unauthorized paparazzi shots. Zeta-Jones called the paparazzi snaps 'sleazy' and 'offensive', and took issue with shots showing her new husband spooning cake into her mouth. Meanwhile, *OK!* sued *Hello!* for breach of confidentiality. Six years later, the England and Wales Court of Appeal (Civil Division) ruled in favour of *OK!* over *Hello!* The court treated the photographs as akin to trade secrets for the purposes of the law of confidences. The argument was that the unauthorized photographs by *Hello!* were taken in breach of confidence since the wedding guests had been clearly informed that they were not permitted to take photographs. Furthermore, there was explicit recognition of a right to privacy by Lord Justice Sedley that English law 'can recognize privacy itself as a legal principle drawn from the fundamental value of personal autonomy' (Goldberg *et al.*, 2009, p. 236).

The House of Lords had earlier, in *Campbell* v. *Mirror Group Newspapers Ltd* [2004], confirmed the legitimacy of the new privacy right in the UK, with a ruling that a newspaper had breached supermodel Naomi Campbell's right to privacy when it published a correct statement that she had visited Narcotics Anonymous. Under the European Convention of Human Rights, an individual's Article 8 rights are engaged if one has a 'reasonable expectation' of privacy in the information concerned.

Balanced with Article 10, the right to freedom of expression, the majority (Lords Hope, Carswell and Baroness Hale) upheld Campbell's claim that her privacy had been breached in the disclosure of private information (her drug addiction, that she was receiving treatment at Narcotics Anonymous, details of that treatment, and a photograph of her leaving a particular meeting) (ibid., p. 238).

In Australia there is no specific statutory privacy 'tort' or wrong defined in legislation. So while jurisdictions in the US and Canada have legislated for a tort of invasion of privacy since the 1970s and, while the courts in the UK do not recognize a tort by that name, the equitable action for breach of confidence has been used in practice to address the misuse of personal information. The New Zealand courts have also recognized the existence of a common-law tort of privacy. But privacy in Australia has arisen as a patchwork of laws and regulations, and several broad categories of privacy tend to get collapsed together to offer protection for:

- personal information or data protection (data held by corporations and government);
- communications (telecommunications interception, the use of 'listening devices' and other types of surveillance devices);
- invasions of private space (autonomy against intrusion into private lives).

In other words, as Australia does not have a uniform common-law right to privacy, privacy is instead protected through a collection of laws. As Butler and Rodrick argue, 'privacy is an umbrella term that may embrace within its ambit matters of privacy of information, privacy of communications, and personal privacy' (2007, p. 384). However, there is continuing pressure to introduce a tort of privacy, especially in the wake of the phone-hacking scandal.

Yet some media events resonate loudly across different common-law jurisdictions, legal systems and cultures. For example, in the wake of the death of Diana, Princess of Wales in 1997, the breach of personal privacy is arguably the issue that most highlights the media's perceived lack of ethics. We can recall the many very memorable scenes of Diana running from paparazzi. Those deeply mythologized images are now embedded in popular consciousness: however, it wasn't a fairy-tale ending as we know – the Diana car-crash video brought in breaking news to our screens that was absolutely shocking. The role of the media was open to scrutiny, and the sharing of intimate private details of the death of the Princess, was for many, evidence of a new level of media privacy transgression.

Privacy at Common Law in Australia

Privacy concerns raised against certain egregious media practices frequently involve complaints by individuals about intrusion into their private affairs by a media outlet: usually involving the publishing of information and/or images without the individual's permission.

While there is some indication that the Australian courts may introduce a common-law right of privacy if a suitable case came along, in the mean time attempts are routinely made to invoke the laws of defamation, confidential information, trespass and nuisance as a means to complain about the actions of the media that interfere with people's expectations (or assumed right) to be left alone. The discussion of privacy law in Australia can tend to become rather murkier because of the existence of information-privacy legislation (or, as it is known in the UK, data protection) at the state and federal levels. There are anti-surveillance laws, which can be added to the mix too.

In Australia, interest in the potential for a tort of privacy was renewed with the High Court decision in *ABC* v. *Lenah Game Meats* [2001] HCA 63. A common-law tort of right to privacy was foreshadowed by some members of the court. In this case footage was obtained from an unknown source using cameras concealed in the ceiling of an abattoir that processed game meat for export. The film, depicting the slaughtering of brush-tailed possums, was supplied to the Animal Liberation organization, which in turn passed it on to the Australian Broadcasting Corporation to be used in a current-affairs television programme. The abattoir sought an injunction to prevent the broadcast of the footage. The Supreme Court of Tasmania refused an interim injunction, later granted by the Full Court. On appeal to the High Court, ABC succeeded by a majority (5–1) to have the injunction lifted. One of the arguments by the complainant/plaintiff was that the acquisition of the footage amounted to an invasion of its privacy. Despite rejecting the application for an injunction, the High Court expressed the view that, in the future, it may be receptive to arguments that a right to privacy should be recognized in Australia. The court considered that such an action may be available where the personal affairs of another are intruded upon; the matter made public is highly offensive to a reasonable person; and there is insufficient public interest in having the information disclosed. English breach-of-confidence principles were considered, but the majority did not believe they should be extended to the filming of private activities (Pearson and Polden, 2011, p. 392).

More recently, another case has reignited the debate over the possibility of a common-law tort of a right to privacy, without it reaching that threshold. In *Giller* v. *Procopets* [2008] the Victorian Supreme Court of Appeal considered an action for breach of privacy arising from the publication of a video of sexual activity. Alla Giller and Boris Procopets had been living in a long-term relationship. Essentially the case was a bizarre family-law-styled dispute that included issues of property law and the law of equity (via a breach of confidence for the release of the video). The appellant, Alla Giller, in her statement of claim, alleged that, in distributing and threatening to distribute videos and in making statements to others about their sexual relationship, Boris Procopets engaged in conduct calculated to degrade and humiliate her and cause her emotional distress. Procopets had thereby committed, so it was alleged, 'the tort of intentional infliction of emotional distress' (Australasian Legal Information Institute, 2011).

Counsel for Alla Giller argued that the trial judge had erred by failing to consider authorities that supported the development of a tort of invasion of privacy in Australian law. Basically, the appeal judges ruled that it was not necessary to decide this issue because Giller had a right to compensation on other grounds – so they didn't need to consider whether a tort of invasion of privacy should be recognized by Australian law.

But in arriving at this position, it was noted that in recent years, two main approaches have emerged in response to claims that English, Australian and New Zealand law should recognize such a tort. The first, epitomized by *Lenah*, has been to develop existing causes of action to provide greater legal protection for privacy interests. It was noted that English courts have not yet recognized an 'over-arching, all-embracing cause of action for invasion of privacy' but, as *Campbell* v. *Mirror Group Newspapers Ltd* and *Douglas and Ors* v. *Hello! Ltd* show, the Human Rights Act 1998 (UK) and the European Convention of Human Rights have provided the impetus for expansion of the cause of action for breach of confidence, to furnish remedies to people who complain of the publication of certain private matters.

The Victorian Court of Appeal argued that the second approach is exemplified by the decision of the New Zealand Court of Appeal in *Hosking* v. *Runting* (2005) to recognize a new tort of invasion of privacy. In that case, by majority, the NZ Court of Appeal held that the tort would be committed by the publication of facts about the private life of a person, where the publicizing of such facts would be considered 'highly offensive to an objective reasonable person'. Justice Gault rejected the approach of expanding the duty of confidence, saying:

> Privacy and confidence are different concepts. To press every case calling for a remedy for unwarranted exposure of information about the private lives of individuals into a cause of action having as its foundation trust and confidence will be to confuse those concepts.
>
> (*Hosking* v. *Runting* [2005] 1 NZLR)

It will be becoming apparent that privacy, though often a concept that is difficult to pin down, is protected through various different laws and codes, and its treatment will therefore vary across legal and cultural contexts.

Other Laws with Privacy Dimensions for Media Practitioners

Confidentiality

As discussed above, the expansion of the cause of action for breach of confidence, to provide remedies to people who claim to have had their privacy breached is grounded in a long history of case law.

Traditionally at common law there's a threefold test for breach of confidence:

1 The information has a quality of confidence; it's the kind of information that is intrinsically 'confidential' and not in the public domain.
2 The circumstances have given rise to an expectation of obligation of confidentiality, either express or implied. The words 'this is confidential' are not crucial in this regard. The terms of a contract might be relevant here, or conditions of employment.
3 The recipient discloses the information (or threatens to), or uses it detrimentally.

(Pearson and Polden, 2011, pp. 289–90)

Defences are available for breaches of confidence, including demonstrating just cause or excuse, legal compulsion on the basis that it was required by law and possible public-interest-styled defences if the breach constitutes a 'fair report' or a 'protected disclosure'.

However, it needs to be recognized that, because the law of 'confidentiality' traverses a range of informational categories from private conversations, commercial or governmental 'secrets', its application to situations involving a claim for personal *privacy*, is at best, rather murky.

Trespass by the Media

It is more than a little ironic that, at a time when technological devices enable the media to intrude into, and digitally capture, the private activities of individuals, it is recourse to some very ancient English common law that may bring a halt to these intrusions.

Essentially, at common law, a person who has the title to land, which the media wishes to enter for the purposes of recording or filming an interview, has a legal right to prevent that occurring. Should it occur without the landowner's permission, they will generally have a right to compensation, and a court may grant an injunction to stop such trespass in the future. However, in everyday news-gathering, this law has failed to help people making a complaint against intrusion by the media.

This is because the pragmatics of many news-gathering exercises mean that film crews, journalists and other people making media stories, can get around these restrictions by obtaining their images or sound while on public ground, or from a position nearby. A number of cases indicate the difficulties involved in restricting media access. For example, in *Bernstein* v. *Skyviews Ltd* [1978] QB 479 Lord Bernstein was unable to prevent aerial photography of his grounds (although the court acknowledged that constant surveillance may amount to a form of nuisance) (Robertson and Nicol, 2008, pp. 312–13). Another famous case is *Victoria Park Racing Co.* v. *Taylor* (1937) 58 CLR 479 where the media circumvented the owner's attempt to gain an injunction because, again, the media were not actually on the owner's land.

For media practitioners an easy way to avoid an action for trespass is to gain the consent of the landowner. If permission is not granted, then there may be other ways to go about making the media story.

Judicial Proceedings

There are myriad laws putting the brakes on the free reporting of the private details of a range of people, with children being the main group protected.

Typically, media practitioners can be fined for breaching a law forbidding the identification of juveniles involved in court cases. This is usually seen to be subsumed within the broader category of contempt laws.

In the UK in 1997 the Court of Appeal found that it would only be on rare occasions that cases involving children would be heard in open court. Following this, in 2002, the European Court of Human Rights stated that it was consistent with Article 6 (1), and exceptions to the principle of open justice, to have an entire class of cases removed from hearings in public, subject to the discretion of the court (Robertson and Nicol, 2008, p. 476). Ofcom's Broadcasting Code of Practice provides a strong advisory in relation to programmes dealing with children ('the under 18s'):

> 1.9 When covering any pre-trial investigation into an alleged criminal offence in the UK, broadcasters should pay particular regard to the potentially vulnerable position of any person who is not yet adult who is involved as a witness or victim, before broadcasting their name, address, identity of school or other educational establishment, place of work, or any still or moving picture of them. Particular justification is also required for the broadcast of such material relating to the identity of any person who is not yet adult who is involved in the defence as a defendant or potential defendant.
>
> (Ofcom, 2011)

This kind of restriction articulates a commonsense ethical response more directly targeted to the vulnerability of children than many similar media codes of practice. However, media practitioners need to be aware that the multiple laws that limit media reporting can often be very detailed.

Nuisance

A person who owns or occupies a property can take action against those who unreasonably interfere with the 'quiet use and enjoyment' of the property. An injunction may be granted against a media organization to stop the interfering conduct and damages may also be awarded. Potential activities that may be affected by the law of nuisance include stakeouts, or blocking access. Persistent telephone calls from a media practitioner seeking to obtain a comment may be regarded as nuisance. A helicopter hovering over a residence may also be a nuisance. The Australian television comedy and satire team The Chaser has fallen foul of this particular law on numerous occasions. In 2009 it had similar legal issues with the Vatican state in Italy after flying a five-metre long blimp over the no-fly zone of the Vatican city state.

Data Protection and Information Privacy

In the UK, information laws under the Data Protection Act 1998 and the Freedom of Information Act 2000 set out the broad parameters regulating the way in which 'data controllers' manage the personal information of 'data subjects'. This development arose following pressure from the introduction of a European *Directive on the Protection of Individuals with Regard to the Processing of Personal Data and on the Free Movement of Such Data* (Directive 95/46/EC, 24 October 1995). The Directive recognizes the right to privacy in the European Convention for the Protection of Human Rights and Fundamental Freedoms. These laws, then, enshrine safeguards and individual rights in the way personal data is processed and distributed, particularly in computerized contexts, but also in more mundane non-computerized instances. In Australia similar laws in the Privacy Act 1988 and the Freedom of Information (FOI) Act 1982 (including the amended act in 2000) mainly concern how organizations handle personal information. In both countries these laws have a single regulator, an 'Information Commissioner' (created in Australia from 2010 as the Office of the Australian Information Commissioner and incorporating the previously separate Office of the Privacy Commissioner) to oversee the administration of these laws.

Data-protection or privacy laws protect how personal information or data are used and managed by the government departments and agencies, and certain private-sector organizations. There are specific rules and principles regarding how information or data concerning individuals may be collected, used and stored, as well as rules covering data quality and security, access and amendment.

Because there are vast computerized data-matching programs these days where information (or 'personal data') given in one context (for example, tax-related data) is cross-matched with social security, or veterans' affairs, etc., the importance of this legal framework should not be underestimated. In Australia the Privacy Act 1988 establishes guidelines about how these activities may be legally and ethically conducted.

The Australian federal legislation, the Privacy Act 1988 and the UK's Data Protection Act 1998 all set out principles for how private organizations and government agencies should manage personal information or data. In addition, in Australia, each state and territory has its own privacy laws or guidelines and some also have separate laws on health privacy. The Data Protection Act 1998 regards 'journalism' (although this is not explicitly defined) as a 'special purpose' (s. 3), and is widely interpreted to generally be exempt from the application of the Act. However, it has been argued that the three leading cases relating to breach of confidence by media organizations, *Campbell*, *Douglas* and *Murray* did rely on the Act, although such claims 'added little practical value' other than 'add to the costs of the litigation'. Yet these commentators also note that for 'those who are not wealthy celebrities, a complaint to the (Information) Commissioner is likely to be far more attractive than facing the costs and risks of High Court litigation' (Goldberg *et al.*, 2009, p. 259).

The Australian federal Privacy Amendment (Private Sector) Act 2000 contains an exemption for journalists in the course of their work as they gather information for news or documentaries for the purposes of making that material available to the public. This exception is given on the basis that the media follow privacy standards. The exemption has operated where the media organization has publicly committed to observe standards that deal with privacy. As private companies, the media fall under National Privacy Principle provisions, and they are granted exceptions under section 7B(4) of the Privacy Act 1988. This covers their news work/information-based programming. The policy intention is designed to balance competing rights, placing a premium on protecting freedom of expression and the importance of the free flow of information to the maintenance of a healthy democracy. The Australian Press Council administers privacy clauses in the Statement of Principles and Privacy Standards for Print Media for the purposes of complying with the Privacy Act 1988. These privacy clauses offer a practical-guidance framework for print-media practitioners in the preparation of publications to observe the 'privacy and sensibilities of individuals'. Moreover, guidance materials also expressly acknowledge that the right to privacy 'should not prevent publication of matters of public record or obvious or significant public interest' (Australian Press Council, 2007). Arguably, the journalists' union, in its code of ethics offers stronger privacy guidance in clause 11: 'Respect private grief and personal privacy. Journalists have the right to resist compulsion to intrude' (MEAA, 1996). The UK's Press Complaints Commission Editors' code of practice has a broadly framed provision for generic privacy rights (e.g. for photography is provides 'It is unacceptable to photograph individuals in private places without their consent'), and specific clauses for harassment, intrusion, children, victims, as well as 'clandestine devices and subterfuge'. The code offers this guidance note for paparazzi photographers: 'Private places are public or private property where there is a reasonable expectation of privacy.' Many of these privacy-related clauses are covered by public-interest exceptions under the code (PCC, 2011).

The ALRC has recommended that the scope of the journalism exemption be clarified, by inserting a definition of 'journalism', which is not currently defined in the Act. It also recommends that for the exemption to apply to an organization, the standards to which the organization is committed must adequately deal with privacy (ALRC, 2008). There were also some calls for refining the terms used to define it because of the difficulties associated with distinguishing journalism from commercial and other activities (especially in the convergent electronic environment). In the ALRC's investigation (see next section) no serious case was presented for the abolition of this exemption.

Typically, in debates about media and privacy laws, a view has been expressed that the role of paparazzi photographers and 'stories about the private lives of celebrities amount to big business, and poor practice would leave media organizations exposed to liability for damages' (ibid.). In this context, many media commentators and practitioners see a general international shift from the right to publish towards the right to privacy. Arguably, as privacy rights increase, the right to publish decreases.

Media practitioners need also to be aware of prohibitions on electronic surveillance. For example, the Victorian Surveillance Devices Act 1999 prohibits the taking of photos and videos in private places and proscribes the use of material from hidden cameras or audio-recording devices. There are similar laws in other Australian states and territories prohibiting the recording of conversations and filming without consent of the parties. It is usually a criminal offence to publish information gathered in this way, and this is the basis of previous and recent 'phone-hacking' scandals in the UK, leading to investigations into the practices of News International journalists.

In police evidence to a home-affairs select committee in 2011, it was argued that in practice, the prosecution of *News of the World* journalists alleged to be intercepting politician and celebrity voicemails, was difficult: it needed to be proven that the intercepts occurred before the voicemails were first heard by the phone's owner. It was reported that this technicality in the law was preventing charges being brought over hundreds of instances of illegal phone tapping by News International journalists (Fenton, 2011).

Privacy Inquiries

A recurring feature of privacy and the media over the past two decades has been the frequency of inquiries seeking to find the best legal frameworks to govern and offer protection to citizens, as our notions of privacy shift over time.

As noted above, unlike in the US, in Australia there is no specific statutory privacy tort or wrong defined in legislation. However, the ALRC, at the culmination of an extensive investigation, has recommended that such a tort be implemented (ALRC, 2008).

Amid concerns about the impacts of more restrictive privacy laws on the 'fourth-estate' role of the media, the ALRC's view was that the courts should be required to consider whether the public interest in maintaining the claimant's privacy outweighs other matters of public interest, including the interest in informing the public about matters of public concern and facilitating freedom of expression. The ALRC's recommended statutory cause of action for *serious* invasion of privacy includes the following types of scenarios:

- After the breakup of their relationship, Mr A sends copies of a DVD of himself and his former girlfriend (Ms B) engaged in sexual activity to Ms B's parents, friends, neighbours and employer;
- Mr C sets up a tiny hidden camera in the women's toilet at his workplace, capturing images of his colleagues that he downloads to his own computer and transmits to a website hosted overseas, which features similar images; and
- Ms D works in a hospital and obtains access to the medical records of a famous sportsman, who is being treated for drug addiction. Ms D makes a copy of the file and sells it to a newspaper, which publishes the information in a front-page story (ibid.).

So while it can be seen that a media organization is directly involved in only one of these scenarios (Ms D), there are processes of mediatization in the other two scenarios through internet distribution (Mr C) or by making DVD copies (Mr A). These are all scenarios that involve media in one way or another: they are worst-case scenarios that few could deny require the strongest available legal frameworks to protect citizens.

Privacy, Communications Technology, Regulation

Privacy issues in the communications sector are becoming increasingly prevalent as new technology and new applications evolve. The rise of social networking and the use of location-based information are prominent examples (De Souza e Silva and Frith, 2012, pp. 111–35). New technology capabilities add to the traditional privacy issues in the sector, arising from spam, telemarketing and the misuse of silent telephone numbers.

No doubt with this in mind, the not-for-profit Australian Communications Consumer Action Network (ACCAN) organization funded a research project undertaken by the Cyberspace Policy and Law Centre at the University of NSW. The purpose of the project was to analyze and compare common communications privacy complaint paths for traditional and new communications media available to people whose privacy has been breached. The premise of the research was that privacy protection in democracies like Australia, or the UK, stands or falls on the efficacy of the available complaints mechanisms.

The report, *Communications Privacy Complaints* (2010) systematically examined complaints made to the Office of the Privacy Commissioner (OPC); to the Australian Communications and Media Authority (ACMA); and the Telecommunications Industry Ombudsman (TIO). The authors found vast differences in complaint resolution times, remedies and compensation available to consumers, depending on which organization dealt with a complaint (Connolly and Vaile, 2010).

In April 2011, a parliamentary Senate Committee inquiry set up to consider privacy implications arising from technical developments such as social networking, online marketing and cloud computing, recommended that the government attempt to resolve the issues raised in the Connolly and Vaille report and related ACCAN advice (Senate, 2011). In the report *The Adequacy of Protections for the Privacy of Australians Online*, the recommendations included: amending the Privacy Act 1988 and the role of the Privacy Commissioner to better respond to complaints made online; to 'develop and impose a code which includes a "Do Not Track" model'; and perhaps of most import, 'that the government accept the ALRC's recommendation to legislate a cause of action for serious invasion of privacy'.

Closed Circuit TV

CCTV usage is an important privacy/data-protection issue involving surveillance technologies and the use of personal information. As CCTV systems proliferate, it has emerged as a legal and ethical hotspot for many societies around the world.

How often do you hear a news report say, 'police are reviewing CCTV footage' to assist in solving a crime? The increasing use of CCTV cameras in public spaces is one of the more visible changes in privacy in recent years. Broadly speaking, their usefulness in reducing incidents of criminal activities has tended to outweigh civil libertarian arguments in relation to growing surveillance trends in society and a general reduction in personal privacy. On the one hand, it is difficult to argue with statistics showing that criminals suspected of very serious crimes (such as murder and rape) have been apprehended after police examination of CCTV footage. On the other hand, however, the police have got it wrong at times, and apprehended the wrong people after relying on CCTV footage. A television current-affairs item, examining the use of CCTV cameras in inner London, illustrated the excessive surveillance now prevalent in cities, when the reporter was captured on camera more than a dozen times as he commuted by bicycle from where he lived to where he worked (ABC, 2007). Another concern is the increasing tendency for surveillance systems to be linked together in cities and for them to be run by computerized systems with little human intervention. As security experts are quick to point out, such systems are only as good as the component elements from which they are constituted. Should one system get it wrong, there is a cumulative 'error' in all the systems.

Confidential Sources and Documents

Confidential sources have always been important to informative media reports, made in the public interest. Confidential sources can be defined as people who provide – while keeping their identities secret – important information that might otherwise not be available to the public.

Historically, only a fairly narrow number of circumstances have qualified as confidential information. They have included trade secrets; computer program ideas; domestic confidences; and tribal, cultural, religious and government secrets. The latter category, government secrets, may trigger disobedience contempt. This occurs when journalists refuse to reveal their sources when asked by a court to do so; in other words, the law of contempt is on occasion relied upon by the state to protect legal proceedings from certain kinds of journalistic practices (Beattie and Beal, 2007, p. 59).

Confidential sources can furnish important information that might otherwise not be available to the public. But when sources leak such information, they often do so at risk to themselves, hence the journalist might promise anonymity to the source in return for the information. In Australia the Media Entertainment and Arts Alliance Code of Ethics (1996) states that journalists must respect all confidences, thus ensuring they keep the trust of those upon whom they depend for information. But if a trial is under way, in which the identity of a source is vital to the case, the judge might decide to call the journalist as a witness to reveal the name of the source.

Since the 1980s, in Australia, without the benefit of shield laws, at least twelve journalists have faced contempt of court charges in Australia for refusing to reveal their sources. The conflict between journalists' protection of their sources and the requirements of the courts remains unresolved. Shield laws are legal mechanisms to safeguard journalists against prosecution, and are available in some jurisdictions to protect journalists in relation to disclosure of their sources. In the US the overwhelming majority of states have shield laws and they are expected to eventually be available at the federal level, having been debated for over six years, although the WikiLeaks saga (discussed below) has now complicated the passing of laws to protect conventional journalistic sources (*LA Times*, 2010). In the UK there is limited protection for journalists under the Contempt of Court Act 1981. This means that in the UK no court

> can require a person to disclose, nor is a person guilty of contempt of court for refusing to disclose, the source of information contained in a publication for which they are responsible unless it is established to the satisfaction of the court that disclosure is necessary in the interests of justice, or national security, or for the prevention of disorder or crime.
>
> (Butler and Rodrick, 2007, p. 329 [7.395])

Put simply, shield laws are laws providing legal protection for journalists who refuse to reveal their confidential sources to a court. Shield laws are based on the premise that it is critically important in a democracy that journalists be able to obtain information to inform the public about matters of interest. Necessarily, this implies that strong protection must be provided to enable the full disclosure of information.

In New Zealand the Evidence Act 2006 contains a specific privilege protecting journalists' sources. In Australia, after a long period of delayed promises, the Evidence Amendment (Journalists' Privilege) Act 2010 was passed in 2011, and as amended, will apply to traditional journalists as well as bloggers and citizen journalists using 'any medium'.

The new laws strengthen provisions relating to information revealed to journalists and require courts to consider whether:

- information was passed contrary to the law in determining whether evidence should be admitted, or whether a source should be revealed; and
- there will be potential harm to the source and/or the journalist if evidence is given.

The laws are modelled on the New Zealand law that provides a rebuttable presumption in favour of journalists not disclosing information in court proceedings that would identify their source. The Act provides that if a journalist has promised an informant not to disclose his or her identity, neither the journalist nor his or her employer can be compelled to answer any question or produce any document that would disclose the identity of the informant.

Many observers stress the important connection between effective shield laws and laws protecting the disclosure of confidential information in the public interest. For example, the Australian Press Council argues: 'the Council has always advocated that the introduction of effective public interest disclosure legislation, that includes provisions for disclosure to the media, also requires the introduction of effective shield laws to allow journalists to protect their sources' (APC, 2010, p. 13).

The interaction between media organizations and sources illustrates the conflict between freedom of expression, the processes of justice and wider public interests. To yield to a court order to reveal a confidence is at the very least to lose face among professional colleagues and, more significantly, to betray a trust. To withhold the information is to deny justice to one or the other party in a case. The courts, generally speaking, tend to respect this conflict and are reluctant to convict, but that has not stopped them from punishing journalists when the administration of justice and ethical media practice were clearly relying on different decision-making frameworks.

Confidential Documents and WikiLeaks

The law protects people's secrets but, as we have discussed above, it has not in the past protected journalists' secret sources. There are, however, crucial differences between the confidential arrangement a journalist might have with a source on the one hand, and confidential documents on the other. For a contemporary blurring of this distinction, we need look no further than the paradigm-changing activities of the WikiLeaks organization in releasing the video 'Collateral Murder' onto YouTube of a US Army Apache helicopter being used to kill innocent Iraqi civilians in Baghdad, including children. WikiLeaks, in the few short years it has operated, has facilitated the disclosure of hundreds of thousands of confidential government and corporate documents into the public domain (Khatchadourian, 2010).

WikiLeaks is arguably the most important story for the public-interest advocacy role of media to have emerged in the last decade. Goggin puts the rise of WikiLeaks in the wider cultural contexts of media, technology and the news industries; as being closely connected with 'wiki' collaborative authoring and editing of documents and, in particular, as representing 'an exemplary if intricate story in how new technologies and the media play out' (Goggin, 2012). WikiLeaks' role as a news organization and publisher however, seems destined to remain shrouded in moral ambiguity (Tiffen, 2011).

If the 9/11 attacks were one bookend signalling the dramatic commencement of the first decade of the twenty-first century, the information bomb that was WikiLeaks can be viewed as the other bookend at the close of the decade. The organization and its head operative, Julian Assange, have been responsible for redefining the concept of whistleblowing, and perhaps even journalism itself, for cyberspace in the twenty-first century. At the centre of this redefinition is the relationship between internet technologies in the Web 2.0 form of a site like WikiLeaks, and the position of legacy news media. At the height of the scandal over the WikiLeaks dump of the so-called 'Afghan war logs', there was remarkable new and old media collaboration between the *über*-leaking organization and the *Guardian*, the *New York Times* and *Der Spiegel*. Under enormous pressure from the US administration, the *New York Times* was able to distance its relationship with WikiLeaks as *only a source* (Fowler, 2011, p. 161).

In fact, these pillars of the established media entered into agreements with WikiLeaks to simultaneously publish their reports regarding the Afghan war logs, at the same time as WikiLeaks released the full dataset on the internet. For the *New York Times* to have described its collaborative relationship as a closer journalistic one may have had far more serious legal consequences under the US Espionage Act 1917, and the US Justice Department's investigation of Assange and WikiLeaks.

Assange apparently made the observation that the *New York Times*'s position could be explained because it may 'need to be not truthful because of threats' (ibid., p. 162). This is an interesting revelation, placing the WikiLeaks' self-definition closer to that of a traditional media publisher, whose fourth-estate role is unquestionably to make information available to the public. The irony in this situation, which was not lost to Assange, was that as a *source* for these major news stories, there would be no journalistic protections offered to either himself or WikiLeaks. Fowler quotes the MEAA's Federal Secretary, Chris Warren as unequivocally judging WikiLeaks as a journalistic enterprise:

> What Assange and his colleagues are doing is journalism, there's no doubt about that ... . One of the most important tasks of journalism is to uncover and inform people of things that other people would rather keep hidden. They've certainly done that.
>
> (ibid., p. 163)

Resource, source or independent media player, WikiLeaks has forever changed the face of what it means to 'blow the whistle', on a scale that was incomprehensible before the arrival of Web 2.0 internet technologies. Assange remains personally at risk from those in the US administration who see his role as akin to espionage, and believe that he should be answerable to the law in those terms.

Journalists face possible legal action if they publish material that has the status of confidentiality. A document does not need to have 'confidential' written on it in order to be confidential – many commercial communications are in confidence. Journalists develop a sense for confidential material; that is to say, they can often identify it even if it is not marked as such. As noted earlier, under the common-law test for breach of confidence, the material must have a 'quality of confidence'; it must have been imparted in a way that carries an obligation of confidentiality. Accidental disclosure of such material is still a breach. To publish is to risk being sued by the party whose confidence has been broken, or to risk being charged with contempt of court if the publication is in breach of a suppression order.

Clearly, then, leaks are the lifeblood of investigative journalism. The person revealing sensitive information usually believes the public has a 'right to know'. But if the leaked material is confidential (and by its nature, it usually is), then any publication carries risk.

Freedom of Information

Freedom of information (FOI) laws are now a characteristic of open government in democratic societies. The key laws in the UK are the Freedom of Information Act (FOIA) 2000 and the Freedom of Information (Scotland) Act (FOISA) 2002. The main commonwealth law in Australia is the Freedom of Information Act 1982. Broad equivalents exist in common-law jurisdictions, although each system has its own specific cultures and features. FOI laws in Australia are mostly based on a US precedent, which has been mirrored in all states and territories except for the Northern Territory. It would be fair to say that all common-law FOI regimes have evolved in response to the pervasive attitude to English Official Secrets legislation 'that government owned official information' (Rolph *et al.*, 2010, p. 707). In this sense FOI regimes awkwardly co-exist with secrecy laws in these common-law jurisdictions.

The US Freedom of Information Act 1966 was inspired by ground-breaking Scandinavian laws (dating as far back as the Swedish Freedom of the Press Act 1766). Freedom of information laws refer to legislation that grants some rights of access to government documents (or a 'public authority' under the UK FOIA 2000) of public interest. Founded on democratic ideals of openness, accountability and responsibility, FOI legislation exists to create an enforceable right to access documents held by governments, their departments and agencies. There are various exempt agencies (for example, in both the UK and Australia, security organizations), as well as specific categories of exempt documents and in Australia these include:

* documents dealing with essential interests or functions of government, such as national security;
* those concerning relations between state and territory governments;
* Cabinet documents;
* Executive Council documents;
* documents that would jeopardize the deliberative processes of government ('internal working documents') against the public interest;
* those relating to personal privacy or personal affairs;
* documents concerning legal professional privilege or judicial functions;
* documents detailing business or trade secrets;
* law-enforcement documents;
* documents that would prejudice a fair trial, breach a confidence or constitute contempt of court.

Even though FOI remains an important channel for access to government information by the media, most users of FOI are non-journalists, seeking access to their own personal information. There are many constraints on the use of FOI laws by media organizations, particularly in relation to speed of access in the context of a twenty-four-hour news cycle, exempt documents and the high costs of requests.

The FOI process is sometimes criticized on the basis of the number of exemptions and the high costs involved, which have tended to thwart its original objectives. However, some media organizations have staff ('FOI editors') who are very skilled at fashioning requests which go beyond random fishing expeditions, and they are able to haul in quite specifically targeted documents, most relevant to a particular investigation.

As an indication of the power of secrecy laws and culture in the UK, while the UK's FOIA was passed in 2000, it was not until 2005 that the key right of access to information under section 1, actually came into force (Goldberg *et al.*, 2009, p. 263). As long as the Official Secrets Acts of 1911 and 1989 remain as central planks of the government's information policies, it cannot be presumed that relatively minor successes, for example, in relation to MPs' expenses, will ensure the long-term survival of FOI legislation.

A controversial feature of Australia's FOI scheme has been the mechanism of a 'minister's certificate', or 'conclusive certificate', which allows a minister to make a declaration that a disclosure of particular documents would be contrary to the public interest. An equally controversial outcome is achieved in the UK by ministerial veto. These kinds of ministerial decisions are beyond the ambit of a full merits review, unlike many administrative decisions made by bureaucracies.

Privacy, Ethics, Social Networking

It is clear that with the rise of Web 2.0 mechanisms (Facebook, Google, YouTube, Twitter), new 'hyper-targeting' technologies using 'ad-serving platforms' constitute a turn in the evolution of commercial speech of media corporations. They are the new media way of corralling and engaging with audiences in the contexts of 'conversational' internet social media. Neoliberal market systems have become increasingly dependent on these kinds of decentred internetworked processes that convert audience activity into marketable data. Accompanying these trends are serious ethical concerns involving the use of personal data. While the US FTC proposes a 'normative framework' for corporations to protect privacy (FTC, 2010), the founder of Facebook, Mark Zuckerberg believes that with the rise of social networking online, people 'no longer have an expectation of privacy', and that privacy is 'no longer a social norm' (Johnson, 2010).

Occasionally, the presumed advantages of new social media for 'linking people up' are placed under the microscope as part of a very public backlash. This was the case when Facebook, the erstwhile brash start-up, and now a very large new media company with almost 1 billion 'active users', including hundreds of millions who use mobile devices to access the platform, introduced a new selling feature called 'Beacon' (Nielsen, 2010; *Financial Times*, 2010). The purpose of Beacon was primarily about advertising, even though it had a veneer of 'social-networking' attraction for its audience users. Free to advertisers, the Beacon feature was not restricted to e-commerce; people getting a high score in an online game could be posted as news for friends on the network.

When introduced in 2007, the idea was that Facebook users' purchases from an affiliated third-party group of more than forty external websites, such as Amazon or Overstock.com, were then broadcast to other Facebook members as 'news'. Implemented originally as a feature with an 'opt out', the pragmatics of doing so were, in the best light, very onerous; users had to visit each Beacon affiliate website and opt out of the program on each site. But it went pear-shaped when the now-infamous Sean Lane's supposedly surprise purchase for his wife of a diamond ring became a Beacon news headline on Facebook: 'Sean Lane bought 14k White Gold 1/5 ct Diamond Eternity Flower Ring from Overstock.com'. The *Washington Post* reported: 'Without Lane's knowledge, the headline was visible to everyone in his online network, including 500 classmates from Columbia University and 220 other friends, co-workers and acquaintances' (Nakashima, 2007). A social-networking feature conceived of as a 'word-of-mouth' promotion tool was actually a new way of marketing that was highly invasive of people's privacy. There was a great deal of grassroots resistance to the commercial exploitation at the heart of the Beacon feature. In a strong show of resistance, approximately 70,000 other users signed a petition organized by MoveOn.org. The text of the petition read: 'Sites like Facebook must respect my privacy. They should not tell my friends what I buy on other sites – or let companies use my name to endorse their products – without my explicit permission' and called on Facebook and similar sites to stop the unauthorized use of members' data (Clark, 2007). In addition, a protest group organized through Facebook groups mustered the signatures of some 50,000 members, as well as formal complaints, including one by the Electronic Privacy Information Center, lodged with the FTC (Cheng, 2007). In a victory for the power of open-source software development, a free plug-in was developed for Firefox designed to completely block Beacon. Facebook CEO Mark Zuckerberg publicly apologized and went into PR flak-control overdrive, admitting that 'a lot of mistakes' had been made (ibid.). Facebook quickly backed down and implemented an active 'opt-in' mechanism for members who agreed to use the feature.

The key privacy concern with the Beacon feature was that Facebook did not attempt to ask any of its users for their consent, as to whether the site could start tracking their non-Facebook activities for broadcast on Facebook. It was clear that Beacon was a vivid instance of social-networking sites introducing more sophisticated advertising for businesses relying on the buying preferences of its membership. As one commentator has noted, advertising is 'the essence of Facebook's business; it's the great and shining hope of that company and social media in general' (Fuchs, 2009). It is difficult to avoid forming the view that this was a media corporation that had overstepped the mark when it came to the privacy limits of these new forms of targeted advertising.

Two years after its unseemly Beacon public relations débâcle, Facebook quietly settled a class-action lawsuit for $9.5 million (Johnson, 2009). The named plaintiffs (about twenty) received $41,000 each. The company agreed to close the Beacon feature in late 2009 and agreed that the money awarded would go towards the setting up of a foundation to promote online privacy (Metz, 2009). A new product, known as 'Facebook Connect', with an opt-in feature, has replaced some of the Beacon features.

But, in addition to these new applications within Facebook, which in themselves raise concerns about data mining and privacy, Facebook strategists have incrementally introduced a number of changes to the settings in order to garner more personal information for marketing purposes. Not surprisingly, this has met with a great deal of user resistance. In early 2010, when users logged onto the site, they were asked to change their privacy settings to those suggested by Facebook. From a limited set of personal information in a user's profile, the suggested default settings now involve all data, personal information, images, fan pages and links being made accessible to all users, not just those people users agree to have in their immediate network of friends. This development, if people agreed to it, could include sensitive personal data as recognized by European Union data-protection laws, such as gender and religious information. Similarly, the American Civil Liberties Union and the Electronic Frontier Foundation were critical of how Facebook managed the situation with little advanced warning or explanation (Gershlick, 2010). One day you log on, you get asked to change some of your preferences (or you left the settings the same, as people more concerned over their privacy rights no doubt did), and before you know it, all your data are available to anyone.

At the risk of stating the obvious, this is a very fast-moving business that requires ongoing public-relations interventions, as technical developments with platforms, especially in the mobile space, demand constant updating and massaging of privacy policies. Facebook users were asked to comment on new proposals with a message announcing that 'updates' were proposed to the site's *Privacy Policy* and *Statement of Rights and Responsibilities*. The message advised that future notifications of proposed changes to the 'Facebook Platform' would appear through the Facebook Site Governance Page and encouraged users: 'to receive future updates to Facebook's site governance documents, become a fan of the page' (Facebook, 2010).

It can be seen that changes are being introduced step by step as Facebook and other social-media corporations like Google with Google+ juggle technical capacities, advertising features and the limits of personal privacy. These ongoing changes come on the back of a system that requires a detached understanding of how personal information is used by Web 2.0 platforms. Facebook users are already required to go through a process of switching default settings set to releasing information they wish to share to 'everybody' (on the web) to 'friends of friends' or to only 'friends'. The platform requires that people actively go through a series of non-transparent steps to protect their privacy in several settings categories: information in profiles, information in posts, personal information and search (ZDNet, 2010). Facebook automatically releases name, picture profile (if one has been posted), list of friends and connections to anyone on the internet. It is just one of many sites that are pushing the envelope, serving up personalized and 'social ads' that these social-networking platforms now enable. Advertisers work closely with these sites, sharing personal information with third parties to identify which people are likely to want particular goods and services represented in commercial or sponsored content. To do this requires personal, and often sensitive, information about individuals and their lives and consumption preferences. It is for this reason that Do Not Track laws have been introduced, and the FTC is developing appropriate online privacy frameworks (FTC, 2010).

Privacy advocates are deeply concerned about these developments and their potential to infringe people's privacy rights (Chester, 2007). The market power to abuse personal information aggregated through usage is unprecedented; it represents the long-held marketing dream of directly threading together the production, distribution and consumption of goods and services. Indeed, the levels of scale and the power of interactivity in new online marketing and advertising have reached an only previously imagined situation – allowing ads so individualized that they are 'selling us ourselves' (McAllister, 1996).

The development of legislation for the protection of users in online advertising environments, where users are liable to have limited, or only complexly negotiated, control of comments, personal data and privacy settings in online media services, is currently concentrating the minds of politicians and government officials in many jurisdictions (see e.g. Kerry–McCain Senate Bill, 2011). That these laws are warranted can be seen in the recent US government investigation into Facebook's unauthorized provision of users' personal details to third-party application providers of Farmville and Texas Hold-em Poker (Steel and Fowler, 2010). Clearly, users are vulnerable parties in terms of the widespread collection, archiving, trade and publication of personal information by international media and communications services. As news media services come to rely more on the integration of user-generated content and interaction, in order to demonstrate and exploit value through user measurement, the protection of user information rights will be an important legislative challenge to ensure the accountability of those services.

New internet media businesses are closely implicated in the performance of neoliberal ideologies and strategies for audience engagement. There is an ongoing contest between commercialized proprietary media content and more participatory affiliation structures of social networking and user-created content provision. Existing limitations on the use of personal data are being pushed back by media corporations as the technical capacities of Web 2.0 platforms, for example as seen in hyper-targeting, are being constantly updated to data mine new commercial opportunities.

Powerful stakeholders in the marketing-media complex continue to shape relations with audience users in commercialized internet media, and this involves ethical issues with privacy consequences. In the neoliberal era, the use of unpaid labour in participatory content provision is restructuring media organizations in ways that are yet to be fully understood. What is clear, however, is that new advertising practices directly targeting individuals become better informed as the databases of our own purchasing habits build.

Ethical Philosophy and Privacy

Ethical philosophy helps us to interpret different meanings and dimensions of privacy. There are those who argue that a right to privacy doesn't make sense because it is best covered in or reducible to other areas of established laws, as we have seen in this chapter. Others argue that a right to privacy is entirely coherent. Perspectives from ethical philosophy can offer critical insight for privacy discussions. For example, a deontological perspective on privacy may tend to highlight human autonomy and dignity (people as ends in themselves), and consequentialist arguments may focus on either greater goods or greater evils, and whether these may or may not maximize social benefits. So a consequentialist, for instance, may defend invasion of privacy if it was for the greater good, while for the deontologist it should be inviolate.

Some may pragmatically suggest that the ideas behind establishing a right to privacy are connected with the notion that the intensity of modern life makes it profoundly important that people have a space to retreat from the world. Following this tack, although media intrusion beyond the bounds of propriety is becoming more common, as a value privacy remains fundamental to human dignity and personal autonomy.

Discussions about the reform of privacy laws tend to recur in the context of some media event. Victimization, exploitation or harassment of innocent bystanders in the pursuit of news are typical examples, but more frequently, we see invasion of privacy of celebrities, as part of the media gossip-scandal machine. On occasions the public interest will outweigh individual privacy, but this usually needs to be judged on a case-by-case basis. The difficulty for governments, regulatory agencies and media organizations is that 'privacy is essentially normative and, as such, the idea of the private changes over time, with part of that change being driven by technological change affecting communications' (Morrison *et al.*, 2007, p. 199). The lives of public figures and celebrities will perennially be the object of media attention, but at the same time, their private lives should be quite reasonably beyond the glare of the media.

Responsible media are able to distinguish between what will interest the public from issues that are of genuine public interest. Professional codes of practice, privacy standards, principles and personal ethical frameworks are there to provide the scaffolding to guide responsible and accountable decision-making. In market societies commercial media will inevitably disrupt an easy application of these frameworks. As we've seen in this chapter, continuously morphing online media are the latest development in the evolution of media industries that are threatening to undermine ethical media practices, on both micro and macro levels. But they are not the only terrain of concern: an overzealous state can do as much harm as privately run corporations. In an information society that is often also a 'surveillance society' the combination of information technologies and the desire by governments and corporations to know more about people (for different motives), will continue to place increasing pressure on the broad and internationally recognized human right of privacy.

References

Australasian Legal Information Institute (2011), available at Austlii.com.edu.au.

Australian Broadcasting Corporation (ABC) (2006) 'Truth, Defamation and Privacy' (television programme), *Media Watch*, broadcast 10 April [on-line], available at http://www.abc.net.au/mediawatch/transcripts/s1613045.htm.

Australian Broadcasting Corporation (2007) *Foreign Correspondent* (television programme).

Australian Communications and Media Authority (ACMA) (2010) *Investigation Report No. 2431, Seven Nightly News, (re Minister David Campbell)*, 23 December, available at www.acma.gov.au.

Australian Law Reform Commission (ALRC) (2008) *For Your Information: Australian Privacy Law and Practice*, Report No. 108, September, ALRC, available at http://www.austlii.edu.au/au/other/alrc/publications/reports/108/.

Australian Press Council (APC) (2010) *Annual Report, No. 34. 2010*, available at http://www.presscouncil.org.au/.

Australian Press Council (2007) 'Privacy Issues', *Australian Press Council News* vol. 19 no. 1 (February), available at http://www.presscouncil.org.au/pcsite/apcnews/news07.html.

Australian Senate (2011) *The Adequacy of Protections for the Privacy of Australians Online*, Australian Senate, available at http://www.aph.gov.au/Senate/committee/ec_ctte/online_privacy/report/b01.pdf.

Beattie, S. and E. Beal (2007) *Connect and Converge. Australian Media and Communications Law* (Melbourne: Oxford University Press).

Butler, D. and S. Rodrick (2007) *Australian Media Law*, 3rd edn (Sydney: Lawbook Company).

Castells, M. (2007) 'Communication, Power and Counter–power in the Network Society', *International Journal of Communication* vol. 1, pp. 238–66.

Cheng, J. (2007) Facebook Reevaluating Beacon after Privacy Outcry, Possible FTC Complaint, *Ars Technica*, 29 November.

Chester, J. (2007) *Digital Destiny: New Media and the Future of Democracy* (New York: New Press).

Clark, A. (2007). 'Facebook Apologises for Mistakes over Advertising', *Guardian*, 6 December.

Clark, G. (2011) 'Do Not Track Laws Gain US Momentum', 6 May, *Register*, available at *TheRegister.co.uk*.

Connolly, C. and D. Vaile (2010) *Communications Privacy Complaints: In Search of the Right Path*, Cyberspace Law and Policy Centre/Australian Communications Consumer Action Network, Sydney.

De Souza e Silva A. and Frith, J. (2012) *Mobile Interfaces in Public Spaces. Locational Privacy, Control and Urban Sociability* (New York and London: Routledge).

European Union (1995) *Directive on the Protection of Individuals with Regard to the Processing of Personal Data and on the Free Movement of Such Data*. Directive 95/46/EC, 24 October, available at http://europa.eu/legislation_summaries/information_society/data_protection/l14012_en.htm.

Facebook (2010) *Privacy Policy* and *Statement of Rights and Responsibilities*, retrieved from Facebook.com.

Federal Trade Commission (FTC) (2010) *Protecting Consumer Privacy in an Era of Rapid Change. A Proposed Framework for Business and Policymakers*, December, US Federal Trade Commission.

Fenton, B. (2011) 'Top Yard Officer Calls for Review of Phone Hack Laws', *Financial Times*, 30 March, available at FT.com/media.

Financial Times (2010) Editorial, 'Facebook at 500 million', 24 July.

Fowler, A. (2011) *The Most Dangerous Man in the World* (Melbourne: Melbourne University Press).

Fuchs, C. (2009) 'Social Networking Sites and the Surveillance Society', Salzburg/Vienna, Austria. Forschungsgruppe 'Unified Theory of Information' – Verein zur Förderung der Integration der Informationswissenschaften, available at http://fuchs.icts.sbg.ac.at/SNS_Surveillance_Fuchs.pdf.

Gershlick, P. (2010) 'Facebook Criticized over New Privacy Settings', *Lexology*, 25 January.

Goggin, G. (2012) *New Technologies and the Media* (London: Palgrave Macmillan).

Goldberg, D., G. Sutter and I. Walden *et al.* (2009) *Media Law and Practice* (Oxford: Oxford University Press).

Goodin, D. (2011) 'Do Not Track Bill Introduced in US Senate', *TheRegister.co.uk*, 10 May, available at http://www.theregister.co.uk/2011/05/10/do_not_track_bill_in_senate/.

Johnson, B. (2009) 'How Facebook Tried to Put a Shine on $9.5m Privacy Suit', *Guardian*, 21 September, available at http://www.guardian.co.uk.

Johnson, B. (2010) 'Privacy No Longer a Social Norm, Says Facebook Founder', 11 January, available at Guardian.co.uk.

Kenyon, A. and M. Richardson (2006) 'New Dimensions in Privacy: Communications Technologies, Media Practices and Law', in *New Dimensions in Privacy Law: International and Comparative Perspectives* (Cambridge: Cambridge University Press).

Khatchadourian, R. (2010) 'No Secrets: Julian Assange's Mission for Total

Transparency', *New Yorker*, 7 June, available at www.newyorker.com/reporting/2010/06/07/100607fa_fact_khatchadourian.

Lindsay, D. (2004) 'Naomi Campbell in the House of Lords: Implications for Australia', *Privacy Law and Policy Reporter* no. 20.

Los Angeles Times (2010) 'WikiLeaks and a Journalism "Shield Law"', Editorial, 5 August, available at http://articles.latimes.com/2010/aug/05/opinion/la-ed-shield-20100805>.

Martínez-Cabrera, A. (2010). 'Technology Leading to More Invasive Marketing', *San Francisco Chronicle*, 8 February.

McAllister, M. (1996) *The Commercialization of American Culture: New Advertising, Control and Democracy* (Thousand Oaks, CA, London and New Delhi: Sage).

McClelland, R. (2011) 'New Shield Laws Mean Better Protection for Journalists', Australian Attorney-General's Department, *Media Release*, 21 March.

Media Entertainment and Arts Alliance (MEAA) (1996) *Code of Ethics*, available at http://www.alliance.org.au/code-of-ethics.html.

Merritt, C. (2007) 'Privacy Law to Hit Press Freedom', *Australian*, 22 March, pp. 13–14.

Metz, C. (2009) 'Facebook Turns out Light on Beacon', *Register*. 23 September, available at http://www.theregister.co.uk/2009/09/23/facebook_beacon_dies/.

Morrison, D., M. Kieran, M. Svennevig and S. Ventress (2007) *Media and Values: Intimate Transgressions in a Changing Moral and Cultural Landscape* (Bristol and Chicago: Intellect).

Nakashima, E. (2007) 'Feeling Betrayed, Facebook Users Force Site to Honor Their Privacy', *Washington Post*, 30 November, available at http://www.washingtonpost.com.

Neale, R. and R. Mason (2009) 'Networking Site Cashes in on Friends', 31 January, available at http://www.telegraph.co.uk.

Nielsen (2010) *Top 100 Sites*, January, available at http://www.nielsen.com.

Ofcom (2011) 'Broadcasting Code of Practice', February, available at http://stakeholders.ofcom.org.uk/broadcasting/broadcast-codes/broadcast-code/.

Pearson, M. and M. Polden (2011) *The Journalist's Guide to Media Law*, 4th edn (Sydney: Allen and Unwin).

Press Complaints Commission (PCC) (2011) *Editor's Code of Practice*, ratified January, available at http://www.pcc.org.uk/assets/111/Code_of_Practice_2011_ A4.pdf.

Robertson, G. and A. Nicol (2008) *Media Law*, 5th edn (London: Penguin).

Rolph, D., M. Vitins and J. Bannister (2010) *Media Law: Cases, Materials and Commentary* (Melbourne: Oxford University Press).

Steel, E. and G. Fowler (2010) 'Facebook in Privacy Breach', *Wall Street Journal*, available at http://online.wsj.com/article/SB10001424052702304772804575558448407523968.html?mod=djemalertTECH.

Tiffen, R. (2011) 'The Imperfect Storm', *Inside Story*, 3 June, available at http://inside.org.au/the-imperfect-storm/.

Turow, J. and L. Tsui (2008) *The Hyperlinked Society: Questioning Connections in the Digital Age (The New Media World)* (Ann Arbor: University of Michigan Press).

US Senate (2011) Kerry–McCain Senate Bill, 'Commercial Privacy Bill of Rights Act of 2011'.

Warren, S. D. and L. D. Brandeis (1890) 'The Right to Privacy', 4 *Harv. L. Rev.* vol. 193.

Williams, C. (2009). Facebook Turns Pollster in Search for Cash, *Register*, 23 February, available at http://www.theregister.co.uk/2009/02/03/facebook_market_research/.

ZDNet (2010) 'Facebook Privacy Settings', video tutorial by Molly Wood, available at http://www.zdnet.com.au/videos/play/22499013/.

5 Intellectual Property and Modes of Regulation

In this chapter we explore the idea of culture as property as the main metaphor that sustains intellectual property (IP) laws: copyright, moral rights, patents, designs, trade marks and 'passing off' in common law. A broad range of IP issues has transformed legacy conceptions of 'how the media works', requiring new thinking about the regimes of moral value that underwrite the commodification of expression. There are several examples to demonstrate this argument: the scale of redistribution of music and television content on the internet; journalists and others who plunder social-networking sites such as Facebook without permission; issues in relation to the manipulation of images using software packages designed for that purpose.

In this very traditional area of intellectual property rights (IPRs), the ability of long-held frameworks to enforce those rights has been undermined by a tsunami of change in the media and cultural industries, first by music distribution on the internet, and then by audiovisual products. IPRs issues place into stark relief, and are a key exemplar of, the pressures that are reconfiguring the regulation of contemporary media and communications. They provide a vivid case study of how media and cultural products are now produced, distributed and consumed under very divergent conditions. The rollout of fast broadband networks is amplifying the pressure for regulatory change.

These industry developments are forcing governments to reappraise the arguments for and against regulating the media. What are the different interests to be balanced in deciding whether to regulate and if so, what kind of regulation is appropriate? What content is often deemed 'offensive' and why? For example, why was the Russell Brand and Jonathan Ross incident on BBC Radio 2 considered offensive? Similarly, why were the pranks of 'Shock Jocks' Kyle Sandilands and Jackie O on commercial radio in Australia seen to be at the outer limits of ethical conduct? What are the specific features of the institutional conditions that shaped these events? How can we usefully evaluate different 'modes of regulation' ('self-regulatory' and 'co-regulatory' codes of practices, and black-letter law or 'bright-line' regulation), and other forms of ethical, professional or 'best-practice' supervision (Black *et al.*, 2007)? How can we explain the operation of different modes of regulation (by the state primarily through 'convergent' regulators like Ofcom and the ACMA), but also other more self-regulatory modes as seen in consumer telecommunications, or in public service or commercial broadcasting, which may only escalate to black-letter law in more egregious instances. However, to set the scene for this broader discussion of the modes of regulation we briefly consider a file-sharing case, which has the eyes of both rights holders and internet content downloaders from around the world on Australia.

The Roadshow Films Pty Ltd v. iiNet Case

This landmark case in 2009–10, involving a Hollywood-studio copyright lobby group representing over thirty film studios and TV broadcasters, the Australian Federation against Copyright Theft (AFACT), suing Australia's third largest ISP, iiNet, was highly illustrative of the state of the contested consumption and distribution of media products over the internet. Media reports tended to describe it as the latest skirmish in the 'file-sharing war'. The action was litigated in the Federal Court in Sydney, but it had global implications for the future of the regulation and policing of copyright. Observers of the high-profile file-sharing case were asking: Although copyright owners in general have a fair claim to seek payments for those who use their content, does this necessarily mean that it is reasonable to attempt to have internet-service providers (ISPs) police what their users actually do with television shows or movies? The plaintiffs alleged that iiNet made no attempt to assist the studios in enforcing their copyright, which it is argued is an important obligation to be eligible for 'safe-harbour' provisions under Australia's 2006 amended Copyright Act (Holt, 2009). As Justice Cowdroy remarked in his judgment, 'In Australian copyright law, a person who authorizes the infringement of copyright is treated as if they themselves infringed copyright directly' (Cowdroy, 2010).

The decision of the Hollywood representative AFACT group to sue a large Australian ISP was significant. There are many ISPs in other countries that approximate iiNet's profile in comparable common-law jurisdictions. Yet with various jurisdictional and subscriber base factors in alignment, based on its research AFACT, chose to commence its action (through the local film company Roadshow Films), against iiNet in Australia for facilitating and/or allowing copyright-infringing downloading of movies and TV shows. A vast swath of all internet traffic is considered to be related to copyright-infringing content, and share software BitTorrent is thought by industry commentators to be the biggest source of illegally downloaded content, accounting for the majority of all peer-to-peer interactions (Tung, 2009). Hence, the broader concern, with industry-wide implications, focused on the claim of authorization liability of internet-service providers, whose customers illegally download copyrighted works using the BitTorrent software.

It was alleged in proceedings that AFACT served tens of thousands of infringement notification letters on the Perth-headquartered ISP, where a decision was made not to forward these on to subscribers. There is enormous pressure for change in the distribution and consumption of media products, and people using large amounts of bandwidth and the industry IP paranoia converged in this case. One of the many challenging legal issues was the difficulty of identifying an individual infringer merely from the ISP address, which s/he used to access the internet. The difficulties were said to arise from, among other things, the fact that infringers can access the internet through other people's wireless internet connections.

The prehistory of this phase of the copyright wars took place over a decade ago, and saw the first legal battles waged by the Record Industry Association of America and the Motion Picture Association of America against distributors of the software used for illegal music file sharing, such as Napster, Grokster and Kazaa. Finding the strategies of targeting file-sharing programs and individual infringers to be generally ineffective, and certainly aware of the negative media-relations story it had created for itself, the Hollywood copyright owners shifted to a new tactic: litigating against ISPs became a new test site for copyright enforcement. It was clear evidence that copyright owners had a view of the internet, and its purposes and capacities, that was completely at odds with how the mass audience now use this infrastructure.

The case was a stark example of old-world media ideas confronting the new media world. In February 2010, a Federal Court judge ruled in favour of iiNet, letting ISPs off the hook for their customers' illegal downloads (Cowdroy, 2010). Twelve months later, the Hollywood film and television production studios represented by AFACT lost their appeal to the full Federal Court (ABC, 2011). The blogosphere was replete with ethical judgment:

> Given the sort of lobbying power we see on this issue (including massive diplomatic pressure from the US), don't be surprised to see legal changes attempted on this issue quite soon. However, politicians

would be wise to heed the points raised in the original decision about the silliness of putting the burden on ISPs rather than the copyright holders – the only ones who actually can reasonably do something in these situations.

(Techdirt, 2011)

The High Court of Australia again found in favour of iiNet in unanimously dismissing an appeal by AFACT. The court observed that 'iiNet had no direct technical power to prevent its customers from using the BitTorrent system to infringe copyright in the appellants' films' (Taylor, 2012). From a policy perspective, the bigger-picture issues relate to the changing dynamics of the digital media industries, in terms of production, distribution and consumption. The transformation of the recording entertainment and media industries can indeed be accurately described as a kind of ' "perestroika" and "glasnost" from below: an economic restructuring and an informational opening up that challenge capitalist relations of intellectual property' (David, 2010, p. 9). But those who question the morality of piracy, and its impact on creative artists' work, are probably not paying attention to the emerging alternative business models which see popular music artists release their recordings directly to their websites, and in that process remediating legacy IP value chains.

Media Practitioners and Copyright

In the UK, the Copyright, Designs, and Patents Act 1988 is the main statute protecting intellectual property. In Australia, the Copyright Act 1968 (Cth) protects all creative and intellectual property. The US has the Copyright Act 1976. In general, the principles underpinning these laws apply across common-law jurisdictions.

Despite the fact that copyright laws operate in national jurisdictions, they have become increasingly globalized through international treaties and international trade agreements. These have the effect of setting minimum standards for rights and providing avenues for enforcement, and trade sanctions in the case of World Trade Organization (WTO) treaties. For example, in Australia, several of the Digital Agenda amendments from 2000, for example, were subsequently repealed and replaced by laws to implement Australia's free-trade agreement with the US (AUSFTA), including the Copyright Amendment Act 2006 (Cth).

However, it can be seen that the influence of international treaties has resulted in the harmonizing of the duration of rights across the main categories of copyright. The transnational agreements include the Rome Convention (1961), Berne Convention (1971), Phonograms Convention (1971), Universal Copyright Convention (1971), Agreement on Trade-related Aspects of Intellectual Property Rights (1994) and World Performances and Phonograms Treaty (1996) (Crook, 2010, p. 405). The impact of this harmonization process has resulted in a seventy-year term (after the death of the author) now being the standard duration for the main categories of copyright-protected works. In the US, the Copyright Term Extension Act 1998 has extended the copyright period for corporate authors to 120 years after a work is created, or ninety-five years after publication, whichever is the earlier (Havens and Lotz, 2011, p. 79). In anyone's language this is a very protracted period of time to lock down and limit public access to culture.

The core concept is that copyright does not protect ideas, only the material form of those ideas (Butler and Rodrick 2007, p. 422). Copyright is automatic: it needs no registration, and while the universal copyright symbol is a warning against misuse, it is not essential. The owner of a work of writing, art, photography, music, poetry, performance or a logo, house plan, design or cartoon is the only person entitled to publish the work for any purpose. Another person or entity may use it only with permission.

The copyright owner in a work has the exclusive rights to:

- reproduce the work (for example, convert it to a digital format);
- publish the work (for example, in a newspaper, magazine or book);
- perform the work in public (at various kinds of public events);
- communicate the work to the public (for example, post it on the internet or make it available to download on mobile phones);
- make an adaptation of the work (to another format/medium).

(Australian Copyright Act 1968 s. 31(1)(a))

These are some useful definitions for media practitioners:

Copyright: the exclusive right, granted by law for a period of time, to control the publishing and copying of a particular publication or artistic work. It does not protect ideas, but only the expression of the idea in a material form.
Intellectual property: a broad term used to refer to intangible 'property' created by the mind.
Creative-commons licensing: a form of licensing that encompasses the spectrum of possibilities between full copyright (all rights reserved) and

the public domain (no rights reserved). Creative-commons licences help owners keep their copyright while inviting certain uses of the owner's work – a 'some rights reserved' copyright.

Open-source licensing: a copyright licence to modify computer software code, generally entailing a requirement to make available to others any modifications that are made.

Technological prevention measure: a device, product, technology or component (including a computer program) that in the normal course of its operation controls access or use of the copyright-protected work; for example, software coding that prevents a CD from being used in a car.

Digital technology represents a challenge to copyright precisely because the Act protects the expression of ideas in particular works, literary, dramatic, musical; and digital technologies reconfigure these forms. Digital technologies also introduce new challenges, for example, building a website using video, images, sounds, links to other websites, text quotes or news items published elsewhere will all require permission from the copyright owner (Forder and Svantesson, 2008).

Goldberg *et al.* argue 'IP, and in particular, copyright, underpins the media industries' creative output' (Goldberg *et al.*, 2009, p. 189). However, most creative and intellectual works are copyright: publication of a line of a song or a paragraph of prose needs permission from the owner.

Examples of expression forms in the media and cultural industries include:

- written material such as books, articles, essays, novels, poems, lyrics, letters, training manuals and reports;
- musical works;
- dramatic works such as choreography, screenplays, plays and mime;
- artistic works such as paintings, drawings, cartoons, graphic art, craftwork, photographs, maps and plans;
- computer programs;
- compilations such as anthologies, directories and databases (note that the selection and arrangement of material may be protected separately from the individual items contained in the compilation);
- cinematograph films (note that the visual images and sounds in a film or video are protected separately from any copyright in works recorded on the film or video, such as scripts and music);
- sound recordings such as CDs and MP3s (note that the particular recording itself is protected by copyright, in addition to, for example, the music or story that is recorded);

- broadcasts of television and radio programmes (note that this is separate from the copyright in the films, music and other material which is transmitted); and
- published editions: publishers have copyright in the typographical arrangement of a published edition (note that this is separate from the copyright in works reproduced in the edition).

The question of who owns copyright is sometimes fairly complicated. Even though you might be the media practitioner creating a product (stories, programmes, websites), this does not necessarily mean you automatically own the copyright. Although there is a general rule that the creator holds copyright, there are exceptions:

- material created by employees as part of their job – copyright is generally owned by the employer;
- some commissioned material (although in the main a photographer working under commission retains copyright in their work); and
- material created for a government – copyright is generally owned by the government.

A key point to remember is that media products are often made by many people, and copyright subsists in different works when they are gathered and assembled together. Within a film or video, copyright can subsist in the soundtrack, designs used in the film and so on. In a television broadcast there is copyright in the film or video programme but also the broadcast itself. In music recorded from the radio there is copyright in the broadcast, the performance and the written score of the song. Therefore, it's important to remember that the rights surrounding a property can be multiple and interconnected.

Some Commonplace Issues

In producing media materials, media practitioners may wish to ask themselves these questions to assist in untangling the copyright implications:

- Is the work protected by copyright? (Important to both the owner and third parties considering making use of that work.)
- Which entity owns the copyright, or has an exclusive licence to use the work? (Important when seeking to take a licence for use

of the material or, as the owner, to license it yourself to a third party or when seeking to commence an action against someone else.)

- Can the copyright material be used in a particular way? Will the proposed use infringe copyright or can an exception or defence be relied upon?

Copyright: Key Points to Note

- Copyright lasts for the lifetime of the creator, and for fifty to seventy years thereafter (and in Australia, twenty years for a patent, ten years for a trademark or five years for a design).
- Copyright can be transferred to another owner by sale or assignment (for example, to a publisher in return for royalties or a lump sum), by inheritance or by licensing for a fixed period.
- Copyright permissions usually incur a fee. Media practitioners should obtain written permission, specifying the nature and extent of the use.

Breach of copyright must involve a *substantial* part of the work. The potentially infringing sections or lines may only make up a tiny part of the whole work, but they may also be a crucial part of that work, and hence they illustrate what the courts could debate as being a substantial part. Not surprisingly, the definition of a substantial amount is often the disputed element of copyright litigation.

While the copyright laws distinguish between commercial and educational use, they do not make any judgment about the quality of the work or the talent of the creator: a bad work of literature has as much significance in copyright as one written by a Nobel Prize-winning author. Copyright laws allow some limited copying of protected materials in certain situations; for example, artistic works displayed in public spaces may allow copying by photography or filming.

Unlike in the US, there is no general fair-use provision in Australia or the UK. Instead, the Copyright Act provides a limited number of exceptions (or defences) to copyright infringement under 'fair-dealing' sections covering the following generic situations:

- research or study;
- criticism or review;
- reporting the news;

- legal advice or judicial proceedings;
- parody and satire (in Australia).

Under Australian copyright law, following an amendment to the Copyright Act in 2006, satire and parody are an exception to infringement. The new provisions apply where a person or organization can demonstrate that their use of copyright material (both works and audiovisual subject matter) is a fair dealing for parody or satire. Comedy teams like Australia's The Chaser can now rely on such material to provide the necessary basis for their own creative work. However, these laws are unable to assist them when copyright owners seek to prevent the use of their intellectual property for unauthorized content. The Chaser's attempt to produce satirical commentary on the Prince William and Kate Middleton royal wedding was a case in point. While understandably disappointed, the team could also see the humour in the decision by Prince Charles's media advisor at Clarence House not to allow Australia's national public broadcaster ABC to provide access to the official broadcast 'feed' of the wedding. At short notice the plug was pulled, apparently after it dawned on the Clarence-House media advisors that the notorious comedy team's alternative commentary on the royal wedding was likely to be completely at the royal family's expense. This was easily achieved by the insertion of a use-specification clause ('in any drama, comedy, satirical or similar entertainment programme or content') in the contract between ABC and the official host broadcaster, the BBC, very late in the negotiation of the broadcast rights, expressly prohibiting use of the visuals for those purposes (Idato, 2011).

Moral Rights

Another category of rights exists for creators of certain copyright-protected works, called moral rights. Moral rights impose separate rights and obligations that are associated with copyright in a work, and accompany copyright if the work is eligible for copyright. As Beattie and Beal explain: 'Moral rights differ from copyright in that they are personal non-economic rights. They cannot be sold or licensed and even if copyright is sold moral rights remain with the creator' (2007, p. 122).

Moral rights require the creator to be attributed whenever their work is reproduced, communicated to the public, exhibited or published. They prevent people from falsely attributing a work, treating a work in a derogatory way or modifying it in a way that is prejudicial to the reputation of the creator. Consent is required for each particular event that may breach the moral rights of a creator. The right of false attribution and the right of integrity relate to derogatory treatment of the work. Under section 80 of the UK Copyright, Designs and Patents Act 1988, certain public performances of an altered treatment of the work, including any being 'communicated to the public', may constitute a derogatory treatment. A treatment is 'derogatory' in section 80(2)(b) 'if it amounts to distortion or mutilation of the work or is otherwise prejudicial to the honour or reputation of the author or director'.

Moral rights apply to authors of literary, dramatic, musical or artistic works and to film directors. Exceptions to the right of not having a work subject to derogatory treatment are somewhat more limited than the list of those entitled under the law as having moral rights. Section 82 of the Act explains that, while employees may not have copyright or the moral right to be identified as author or director of a work, they do have the right not to have their work treated in a derogatory fashion, if they have been publicly identified in the work.

In the UK, as section 79 of the Act explains, the moral right to be identified as an author or director of a film does not apply in the case of a computer programmer, the designer of a typeface or an employee. Defences to infringement of moral rights include situations of fair dealing, or where the work is reporting current events or when the publication is a magazine, newspaper, a collective reference work or when permission had been granted. In the UK, unlike in Australia, moral rights do not arise automatically, and need to be asserted in certain precise forms of words depending on the type of work.

Digitalization and Convergence

The advent of processes of digitalization and convergence has placed enormous pressure on IP laws, and their wider cultural implications for creativity and innovation. User-generated and DIY media creation has altered the balance and expectations of deriving income from intellectual property. The inability of traditional legal concepts to adapt to these processes has led to alternatives to conventional IP laws, for example, in creative-commons and open-source licensing. The UK government commissioned a wide-ranging review of IP laws in late 2010. By May 2011, Professor Ian Hargreaves had reported that the UK's 300-year-old legal framework was well beyond its use-by date, arguing 'The UK cannot afford to let a legal framework designed around artists impede vigorous participation in these emerging business sectors.' The review team's remedy, recognizing the need for change in the creative industries, recommended transition measures to 'more open, contestable and effective global markets in digital content and a setting in which enforcement of copyright becomes effective once more' (Hargreaves, 2011). But as the UK's fourth review of IP laws in six years, the ability of the reform case to respond quickly must be in some doubt.

In response to obligations under Article 11 of the World Intellectual Property Organization (WIPO) Copyright Treaty 1996 to introduce technological prevention measures (or TPMs), Australia introduced its own digital copyright laws with the Copyright Amendment (Digital Agenda) Act 2000 (Cth). This Act updated copyright laws for digital media and communications by introducing a 'broad-based technology-neutral' right of communication to the public, which both subsumes and extends the previous broadcast and cable rights. The US Digital Millennium Copyright Act 1998 was the first cab off the rank in this process of updating copyright laws for the digital era.

Broadly, the purpose of these laws was to introduce tougher restrictions on (including to criminalize) consumers' use of digital products such as recorded music and film (David, 2010). So-called 'digital-rights management' and specific TPMs have attempted to limit widespread infringement. This regulatory climate initially fostered a number of high-profile cases in the US and Australia in relation to peer-to-peer (P2P) music and film file sharing. Overall, however, it is evident that the effects of these cases on creation, distribution and consumption media trends have been very limited. Despite a great deal of commentary to the effect that these changes signal the end of intellectual property as we've known it, corporations continue to invest a great deal of money, time and energy in fighting these battles, as we've seen in the earlier discussion.

Yet governments too are seeking new ways to legislate and to enforce existing regulatory schemes. The New Zealand parliament has recently introduced an amendment to the Copyright Act 1994 (NZ) to introduce a 'three strikes' policy towards infringing file sharing. The new law introduces a fine of NZ$15,000 or disconnection from the internet for up to six months for repeat copyright infringers for file sharing. The Copyright (Infringing File Sharing) Amendment Act 2011 (NZ) sets up a tiered system of infringement notifications allowing copyright owners or their agents to notify New Zealand 'Internet Protocol Address

Providers' (or internet-service providers) for infringing activity that occurs on their networks (Pascarl and Akbarzadeh, 2011).

In a similar vein, in 2010 Ofcom released a draft code called the 'Online Copyright Infringement Initial Obligations Code' for consultation purposes. Ofcom has prepared the draft code to give effect to measures set up under the Digital Economy Act (DEA) 2011 to reduce online copyright infringement. The DEA conferred duties onto Ofcom by inserting new sections (124A to 124N) into the Communications Act 2003. As in the New Zealand amendment, the DEA places obligations on ISPs (with more than 400,000 subscribers) to send notifications to subscribers when they receive information from copyright owners. ISPs are also required to record the number of reports made against their subscribers and provide copyright owners on request with an anonymized list of those reports. The new code requires Ofcom to appoint an independent person to determine subscriber appeals (Ofcom, 2010, Para. 7.2). The code requires approval from the UK parliament (ibid., Para. 9.11–9.12).

Creative-commons Licensing

For the long term, how can this apparent impasse be resolved? One very powerful critique comes from the creative-commons movement and Lawrence Lessig, and his ideas connecting innovation, IP and a creative information commons with creative-commons licensing (Lessig, 2005).

New measures connected with circumvention of technology have caused a great deal of concern because of the way in which they have been heavy-handedly applied. At the same time, extensions to the period in which copyright is held to exist, and extension of copyright to any kind of copying, as well as reduction of fair dealing and fair use, means that copyright is today bound up with a regime of regulating creativity.

In Lessig's view, the 'copyright warriors' continue to frame the debate 'at the extremes – as a grand either/or; either property or anarchy, either total control or artist won't be paid'. However, in his view, and it is a persuasive argument, 'the mistake here is the error of the excluded middle'. What is actually needed, he suggests, is 'neither "all rights reserved" nor "no rights reserved" but "some rights reserved" – and thus a way to respect copyrights but enable creators to free content as they see fit' (ibid., p. 277).

Creative-commons (CC) licences build on an open-source concept to define different kinds of rights. It's become a key debate with the rise of internet publishing. The creative-commons position is that, rather than take an 'all rights reserved' approach (a phrase often seen at the end of a film, for example), or a 'no rights reserved', they take a 'some rights reserved' approach. The creative-commons project is not about a copyright-free world, or total control, but rather about leaving certain uses open for creative works while protecting others. Creative-commons licences allow 'the world to distribute, display, copy, and webcast your work, provided they abide by certain conditions of your choice'. The creative-commons organization puts it this way: 'The combination of our tools and our users is a vast and growing digital commons, a pool of content that can be copied, distributed, edited, remixed, and built upon, all within the boundaries of copyright law.' Creators of content can specify that the work must be attributed, or that it is not for commercial use; or that there be no derivative works, meaning that they can't alter or transform the work. Six different creative-commons licences offer a sliding scale: the most restrictive permits redistribution with attribution, while the least restrictive allows redistribution and modification of the work, including for commercial purposes, as long as the original creator is acknowledged (Creative Commons, 2011).

Creative-commons licences have another important feature, which is called 'share alike', meaning that the work can be used, providing that the user makes it available on the same terms. The vision driving the creative-commons project is that eventually people will be able to search for non-commercial songs, and the digital code of the copyright licence will be picked up by search engines. Furthermore, the vision is concerned with 'realizing the full potential of the Internet – universal access to research and education, full participation in culture – to drive a new era of development, growth, and productivity' (ibid.).

Modes of Regulation

In order to extend our understanding of the way law and ethics interact in our media systems, it's important to get a sense of the different *modes* of regulation. The suggestion here is that the *ethics of regulation* itself is important, and it allows us to consider issues such as the effectiveness or otherwise of codes of practice. Questions regarding the independence and transparency of the regulator become paramount in this regard. In this part of the chapter we will be examining the arguments behind different forms of regulation.

Transformations in our media and cultural industries constitute the backdrop against which our analyses of regulation need to be constructed. These changes, now typically characterized as part of the process of 'media convergence', have formed a part of the regulatory landscape for several years (Dwyer, 2010, p. 14). Regulatory agencies throughout the world have restructured their organizations to better respond to these evolving industry conditions.

In Australia, a federal government review of convergence, was conducted from 2011–2012, has forced a reassessment of the most appropriate modes of regulation for different intervention strategies. As one of the first steps in the review, the government released a 'framing paper' to kickstart the debate, with the chairman of the convergence review committee noting that, with profound changes in the media and communications industries set to continue, a review of the main policy frameworks and objectives was urgently required (DBCDE, 2011, pp. 2–3). The argument was that there are a number of ways the government can achieve its specific policy objectives, (such as ensuring a diversity of voices in news and information), including 'regulatory and non-regulatory approaches such as incentive/reward systems' (ibid., p. 3). Let's consider some of these main approaches for intervention in the regulation of our media and communications industries, and also consider recent examples of how these systems work in practice.

Self-regulation

Wilding has provided an analysis of self-regulatory processes in the media and communications industries (Wilding in Nightingale and Dwyer, 2007, p. 269). Self-regulation is sometimes referred to as 'light-touch' regulation. Rules are formulated at least partly by industry participants, and are embodied in instruments. The point is often made by critics that this 'insider design' can lead to limitations in this system of regulation.

Self-regulation is usually shorthand for codes of practice, which the industry sector has some responsibility for maintaining, updating and enforcing. Examples of 'pure' self-regulation include, for example, in Australia, the Direct Marketing Code of Practice, the Australian Association of National Advertisers' Code, or the Press Council's Statement of Principles; or the equivalent body in the UK, the Press Complaints Commission and its Editors' Code of Practice. It is worth noting that this mode of regulation never implies an absence of law: even self-regulation takes place within a context of the application of general media laws.

Co-regulation

Often what people think of as 'self-regulation' is in fact, a form of 'co-regulation' (ibid., p. 269). Co-regulation is usually characterized by the participation of the regulator in formulating the code with industry actors, in addition to a supervisory role, involving the registration of the code. For example, Australia's ACMA sector codes have to be 'approved' under the main broadcasting laws outlined in the Broadcasting Services Act, 1992. In the UK, Ofcom, guided by the Communications Act 2003, plays a similar supervisory role for sector codes.

This means that, in the first instance, industry participants will usually take on the enforcement role and will respond to complaints. But these codes all have some capacity for the regulator to intervene in cases of serious breaches or code failure.

The arguments in favour of this form of regulation are that: it potentially avoids inappropriate use of high-end enforcement options for relatively minor infringements; it is less costly to administer; and it enables those familiar with the fast-changing industry to participate directly in the rule-making. On the other hand, arguments against co-regulation and its perceived ineffectiveness include that: it allows certain matters to be moved 'off the books' of government, while at the same time preserving the impression of regulatory activity; and it allows the industry to protect itself from more necessary direct legislative intervention.

The last twenty years have predominantly been characterized by co-regulatory forms of regulation, which have followed the political economic *Zeitgeist* of *deregulation*. A recent comparative review of audio-visual regulation in multiple liberal democratic jurisdictions (the UK, Germany, Canada and the US) noted that 'All countries have independent or industry bodies that are involved in audiovisual media regulation via self- or co-regulation; these may relate to traditional broadcasting or new media' (ACMA, 2011). Embedded in neoliberal philosophies, deregulation asserts the supremacy of 'the market' as the best mechanism for governance.

Systemic Failures

One of the main purposes of government regulation is to prevent the distribution of material deemed 'offensive', and a code of practice devised by an industry sector and overseen by a guiding regulator is often the most practicable arm's-length way of doing it. If we accept the proposition that governments should be responsible for regulating the media, but then recognize that to make enforceable and detailed laws governing every situation is impracticable, then an alternative approach is required.

Undoubtedly, there are risks to co-regulatory frameworks posed by commercial media scandals, as seen in Australia's high-profile *Commercial Radio Inquiry* of 2000 ('Cash for Comment') where the regulator found: 'A systemic failure to ensure the effective operation of self-regulation particularly in relation to current affairs programs including a lack of staff awareness of the Codes and their implications' (ABA, 2000, Finding 2, p. 4).

Codes of practice have become the *de rigueur* solution. But we can reasonably ask: How well does this approach actually deal with the full spectrum of transgressions, from relatively minor to significant breaches with high-stakes consequences?

This chapter has mapped out some of the main contours of contemporary media regulation: from very directive, unambiguous bright-line laws, which attempt to protect copyright owners in the face of dramatic industry change, to a prevailing mode of regulation that attempts to be simultaneously universalistic and 'light touch'.

Unethical excesses of a commercial market system can result in dramatic failures in these modes of regulation. Yet system-wide choices have been made that claim greater public benefit to flow from market-based regulatory mechanisms. Clearly, there are bigger-picture ideological frameworks that underpin these moral priorities: in *A Brief History of Neoliberalism*, David Harvey defines neoliberalism as based on an idea that 'the social good will be maximized' by 'bring[ing] all human action into the domain of the market' (2005, p. 3).

Creative-commons licensing, derived from the open-source model of software for public access, is not in the first instance about enforcing individual (and corporate) commercial property rights as they are in copyright law. Creative-commons licensing is at its heart a system concerned with regimes of regulating creativity with an eye to a broader set of interests. Similarly, modes of regulation that power share between industry and state actors are concerned (to varying degrees) with *the public interest*, and in the next chapter we consider this important ethical concept more closely.

References

Australian (2009) 'The Year of Living Dangerously', December.

Australian Broadcasting Authority (2000) *Commercial Radio Inquiry: Final Report of the Australian Broadcasting Authority*, August, Sydney, ABA.

Australian Broadcasting Corporation (2011) 'iiNet Wins Illegal Download Appeal', *ABC News online*, 24 February.

Australian Communications and Media Authority (2009) Media Releases, 102/2009, 178/2009.

Australian Communications and Media Authority (2011) *International Approaches to Audiovisual Content Regulation – A Comparative Analysis of the Regulatory Frameworks*. Occasional Paper, May, ACMA.

Australian Copyright Council (2003) 'Ideas: Legal Protection', Information Sheet G15, October, available at http://www.copyright.org.

BBC News (2009) 'Ross TV Return Is Watched by 5.1m', *BBC News*, 24 January, available at 2009. http://news.bbc.co.uk/2/hi/entertainment/7849582.stm.

Beattie, S. and E. Beal (2007) *Connect and Converge: Australian Media and Communications Law* (Melbourne: Oxford University Press).

Black, J., M. Hopper and C. Band (2007) 'Making a Success of Principles-based Regulation', *Law and Financial Markets Review* vol. 191.

Booth, J. (2008) 'Russell Brand Resigns as Radio Host over Lewd Calls to Andrew Sachs', *Sunday Times*, 28 October.

Butler, D. and S. Rodrick (2007) *Australian Media Law*, 3rd edn (Sydney: Lawbook Company).

Copyright Act (1968) Consolidated version of the Copyright Act 1968 (Cth), with Amendments under Both the Copyright Amendment (Digital Agenda) Act and the Copyright Amendment Act 2006 (Cth), available at www.austlii.edu.au/au/legis/cth/consol_act/ca1968133/.

Cowdroy, J. (2010) *Roadshow Films Pty Ltd* v. *iiNet Limited* (No. 3) [2010] FCA 24, available at http://www.austlii.edu.au/cgi-bin/sinodisp/au/cases/cth/FCA/2010/24.html?query=%5eiinet.

Creative Commons (2011) The Creative Commons website, available at http://creativecommons.org/learn/aboutus/.

Crook, T. (2010) *Comparative Media Law and Ethics* (London: Routledge).

David, M. (2010) *Peer-to-Peer and the Music Industry: The Criminalization of Sharing* (London: Sage).

DBCDE (2011) *Convergence Framing Paper*, Department of Broadband Communications and the Digital Economy, June.

Dwyer, T. (2010) *Media Convergence* (Maidenhead: McGraw-Hill/Open University Press).

Forder, J. and D. Svantesson (2008) *Internet and E-commerce Law* (Melbourne: Oxford University Press).

Goldberg. D., G. Sutter and I. Walden *et al.* (2009) *Media Law and Practice* (Oxford: Oxford University Press).

Hargreaves, I. (2011) *Digital Opportunity: A Review of Intellectual Property and Growth*, Intellectual Property Office, available at http://www.ipo.gov.uk/ipreview.htm.

Harvey, D. (2005) *A Brief History of Neoliberalism* (Oxford: Oxford University Press).

Havens, T. and A. Lotz (2011) *Understanding Media Industries* (Oxford and New York: Oxford University Press).

Hitchens, L. (2008) *Media Report*, ABC, Radio National, 28 June, available at http://www.abc.net.au/rn/mediareport/stories/2008/2288031.htm.

Holmwood, L. (2009) 'BBC Fined £150,000 over Russell Brand and Jonathan Ross Phone Prank Scandal', *Guardian*, 3 April, available at http://www.guardian.co.uk/media/2009/apr/03/russell-brand-jonathan-ross-bbc-fine.

Holt, J. (2009) 'The War on File Sharing Hits Australia', 17 November, *ZDNet.com.au*, available at http://www.zdnet.com.au/the-war-on-file-sharing-hits-australia-339299541.htm.

Idato, M. (2011) 'Palace Gags the Chaser's Take on Royal Wedding', *SMH.com.au*, 27 April.

IP Australia (2011) available at www.ipaustralia.gov.au/.

Lessig, L. (2005) *Free Culture. The Nature and Future of Creativity* (London: Penguin).

Nightingale, V. and T. Dwyer (2007) *New Media Worlds: Challenges for Convergence* (Oxford: Oxford University Press).

Ofcom (2008) 'The Russell Brand Show, Report of the Ofcom Content Sanctions Committee', available at http://news.bbc.co.uk/2/shared/bsp/hi/pdfs/03_04_09_russelbrand.pdf.

Ofcom (2010) *Online Copyright Infringement Initial Obligations Code*, available at http://stakeholders.ofcom.org.uk/binaries/consultations/copyright-infringement/summary/condoc.pdf.

Pascarl, I. and A. Akbarzadeh (2011) 'Three Strikes Policy for Copyright Infringement Lands in New Zealand: Is Australia Next?', *Lexology*, 30 May.

Robertson, G. and A. Nicol (2008) *Media Law*, 5th edn (London: Penguin).

Taylor, J. (2012) 'iiNet Defeats AFACT in High Court Case', 20 April, available at ZDNet.com.au

Techdirt (2011) 'iiNet Wins Again: Australian Appeals Court Says ISP Not Responsible For Copyright Infringers', *Techdirt.com*, 24 February, available at http://www.techdirt.com/articles/20110224/00490713240/iinet-wins-again-australian-appeals-court-says-isp-not-responsible-copyright-infringers.shtml.

Tung, L. (2009) 'AFACT Also Targeted Internode, Exetel, Optus', *ZDNet Australian Edition*, 12 October, available at ZDNet.com.au.

UK legislation (2012) Copyright, Designs and Patents Act 1988, available at http://www.legislation.gov.uk/ukpga/1988/48/contents.

6 Media Law, Policy and the Public Interest

The ways in which the media are supervised, or 'regulated' as discussed in the previous chapter, by governments, should be a matter of serious concern for all citizens. When media systems are organized and structured on our behalf by governments, there is an embedded morality that democratically elected politicians are ultimately responsible for maintaining. If we care about other citizens and pluralism, and the quality and accessibility of media, then we are recognizing a moral architecture in these infrastructures.

The term 'the public interest' is typically invoked as a defence to what may in its absence be the worst transgressions by the media. For example, we saw this in Chapter 4 with media invasion of the privacy of celebrities and politicians. The media will often argue that the wider public interest justifies dubious practices. Or another example would be when investigative reporting may need to make harsh judgments in exposing corrupt businesspersons or politicians, who may subsequently commence legal actions for defamation.

But the term 'the public interest' is used more productively to make laws and policies on behalf of less able, or more vulnerable audiences, such as children. The importance of these kinds of interventions has long been recognized in broadcasting and telecommunications policy, and in the self-regulation of the press. Another important sense of the term involves law- and policy-making contexts, where 'big-picture' national or cultural constituencies are at stake. For example, for the past century, US regulatory policy has been guided by a public-interest standard to serve 'the public interest, convenience and necessity' (Barnouw, 1956). It simply means that media and communications are regulated by the state to deliver benefits to wider publics. However, in the history of media regulation, it is recognized as a contentious, sometimes contradictory and at times vague and diffuse term (Feintuck and Varney, 2006, p. 75). Those scholars who attempt to define the term generally want to qualify or express dissatisfaction with their efforts, as Denis McQuail has with this definition: 'the complex of supposed informational, cultural and social benefits to the wider society which go beyond the immediate, particular and individual interests of those who commu-nicate in public communication, whether as senders or receivers' (McQuail, 1992, p. 3).

As the title suggests, the focus of this chapter is the intersection of media law, policy and ethical discourses that come together under the rubric of 'the public interest'. The notion of the public interest tends to be emphasized in media and communications courses that are exploring legal and ethical issues in the media. In the context of discussions of policy and regulation, 'the public interest' is generally concerned with the fact that powerful media formations are not held accountable. It's therefore a vital policy and regulatory discourse that has democratic significance concerning media performance. To assist us in engaging in this task of examining contemporary understandings of 'the public interest', we'll consider more closely a particular set of media industry processes and related policies, where the interaction of these is very much in the foreground.

In discussions about the relationship between media and democracy, it's difficult not to take into account closely interconnected issues such as the law and policy frameworks for media concentration and ownership, regulating convergent market structures and public-service media. More specific discussions regarding the actual categories of content, and how people do (or do not) gain access to media content on different platforms, are then activated by questions regarding the broader industrial structure. In this chapter, media-ownership regulation and the future of news content in the media are used as exemplars of key public-interest concerns for policy-makers.

Influential Media

For the past fifty years or more there has been widespread international support for the proposition that plurality in the ownership of influential media is the best way to promote diversity of opinions. Laws that place structural limits on the number of media outlets owned by one proprietor are regarded as a precondition for achieving a diverse range of viewpoints in democratic nations (Baker, 2007). The precise meaning of 'influence' is, of course, problematic. However, in the vernacular of both governance and citizens, it has been considered to mean *able to generate sufficient shared meanings to mobilize policy actors.*

The presumption by legislators and policy-makers is that a concentration of ownership confers undemocratic power on owners to sway governments, and advance their own private interests at the expense of wider public interests. In addition, the terms plurality and diversity have been used in the policy discourses of liberal democratic nation-states to describe the architecture of service provision, and the range of available formats and content genres. It has been assumed that there is a close connection between concentrated ownership, the policies that allow it and the possibility of ethical media practice. It is also clear that there is inevitable conflict between the basic norms of the market (self-interestedness of actors, producers responding to mass 'demand' for product, oligopoly), and the norms of the media (truth is valued, pluralism in viewpoints is a goal). The result is often that narrow commercial imperatives prevail at the expense of broader public interests, hence the need for supervision and intervention (Spence *et al.*, 2011, pp. 68–9).

Despite significant watering down in the strength of these kinds of laws, many nations, including the UK and other EU member states, the US, Canada and Australia, understand their continuing importance, and also place limits on the number of different kinds of traditional media that can be owned by one person or media group.

Major media owners in the twenty-first century, as in the twentieth century, are striving to strategically expand their output across new media platforms (including the web, 3G mobile and tablets), devices and services (Dwyer, 2010). As they endeavour to recoup the costs of research and development in these new technological ventures, they are also restructuring their operations to reduce costs, and seeking to strengthen and extend their relationships with media users to ensure revenue and information streams. The potential problems of a reduced investment in professional journalism and media production are well documented and debated (MEAA, 2010).

It remains to be seen how rapid industry restructuring and parallel changes to audience access and consumption practices will impact on the development of diversity rules by democratic governments. These changes are being grappled with by governments around the world, often in the context of reviewing the implications of convergence on regulation and policy (DBCDE, 2011 and 2012).

Several important factors can be seen at play in these developments:

- Existing traditional media objectives for media diversity and ownership plurality will not evaporate into thin air merely because these industries are evolving.
- The challenge for governments and their regulators is to develop regimes that encourage diversity; are based on enforceable rules in the

public interest; and that prohibit monopolized ownership and control of influential media.

- There are no characteristics inherent in new delivery platforms that suddenly remove the need for such rules, contrary to populist rhetorics about the diversity of the web or democracy of social media.

As internet distribution evolves, and content production and distribution are beholden to commercial logics similar to those that apply to traditional media, existing policy objectives remain important in those countries claiming to have democratic media. Since 'monitory democracy and computerized media networks behave as if they are conjoined twins', their fates are necessarily interdependent (Keane, 2010, p. 739). There are other dimensions to this issue: innovation in funding public-service media is an equally important component in media diversity frameworks. The funding of public-service media is usually premised on forms of public-interest justifications invoking the perceived wider societal benefits for a nation's citizenry.

So established commercial media companies may be seen to be either consolidating or actually extending their influence via new media services and channels. At the same time, many media corporations are reducing their expenditure on the provision of some types of news and information by reusing (including licensing), reversioning (involving updating and minor editorial intervention), repurposing (for mobiles or iPad) and outsourcing production. These trends demonstrate the limits of diversity in convergent media-production environments.

Web forms such as citizen journalism, blogs and social media are frequently put forward as the panacea to fading media diversity. Although the web holds the *potential* for great content diversity, a growing body of evidence shows that it is precisely because of the online dominance of established media groups, that content diversity is not reflected in the way people actually use the net to access news stories. This evidence indicates that people go to the online sites of traditional news outlets, or to news aggregators, branded portals or search engines, which in turn rely on traditional news organization sources (Dwyer *et al.*, 2011).

Therefore, while popular wisdom has it that the internet has ushered in a diversity of voices in news, in a practical or traditional sense, this is largely a mirage. The news that people access on Google News, Facebook and Twitter is dominated by media sources already familiar before the sites in question existed. These online news audiences are expanding as traditional news audiences are in decline.

The populist default response is that regulating these platforms in the public interest would be 'too hard'. Several decades of neoliberal *Zeitgeist* have fuelled that attitude. But from a public-interest perspective, it would be more accurate to say that regulating the new media spaces requires renewed commitments by governments, on behalf of the publics they represent.

The largest regulatory actor in the world, the EU, has not shied away from investigating these new media regulatory frontiers in the public interest. In 2007, the Council of Europe's Committee of Ministers signalled a longer-term project of renovating legacy media-policy rationales, and in reasserting traditional measures for promoting pluralism and diversity. It recommended that member states should consider adopting rules for multiplatform digital distribution by:

- limiting the influence that a single person, company or group may have in one or more media sectors;
- introducing thresholds based on objective and realistic criteria, such as audience share, circulation, turnover/revenue, the share capital or voting rights;
- using rules capable of being applied in horizontal integration phenomena or mergers in the same branch of activity and to vertical integration phenomena (e.g. controlling key elements of production, distribution and related activities such as advertising or telecommunications);
- endowing agencies responsible for regulation with sufficient powers to require divestiture of media assets where unacceptable levels of concentration are reached.

(2007, EU/CM/Rec 2.1–2.6)

These rules for regulating media 'influence' have historically been informed by a central *policy* rationale in media regulation: generally referred to as rules in 'the public interest'. A non-exhaustive list of these rules includes: laws to encourage diverse media ownership (and viewpoints) on behalf of citizens; laws to facilitate competition in the marketplace on behalf of consumers; laws to restrict foreign ownership; laws for local ownership; or laws to protect the interests of young audiences. All these rules could not have evolved to their present form without recourse to this notion.

So how can this rationale of *the public interest* be better understood, when we talk about media law and policy?

The Public Interest and Citizenship

A robust case can be made that 'the public interest' is mainly concerned with the ethical implications for citizenship of power formations of media that are rarely held accountable. It therefore represents a set of vital policy and regulatory discourses that has democratic significance for citizens, and is critically linked with media performance.

There are various definitions of the public interest, ranging from quite straightforward ones encapsulating less explicit ideas of contestation, through to those attempting to explain conflict in terms of more complex and dynamic formations of media power. For Australia's Press Council, 'public interest' is defined as 'involving a matter capable of affecting the people at large so they might be legitimately interested in, or concerned about, what is going on, or what may happen to them or to others' (APC, 2009). At the other end of the spectrum, Sorauf's definition is useful: 'the complex procedures of political adjustment and compromise which the democratic polity employs to represent and accommodate the demands made upon its policy-making instruments' (Sorauf, 1957).

While Sorauf's definition focused on political processes, others have suggested that it offers a way of *mediating* the interests of the mass media and individuals. For example, drawing on the work of Dennis and Merrill, Maras has argued that

> it mediates between the interests of the media as issuer of information, and the interests of the consumer of information. It is a way to harness the press, and structure its responsibilities. This idea of a 'mediating principle' is interesting as it gives us a way to say that the public interest is never fixed but always subject to debate, deliberation and judgment.
>
> (Dennis and Merrill, 2005, p. 162; Maras, 2007)

Not surprisingly, then, it is a term that recurs in the judicial system. Journalists might argue there is 'a public interest' in publicizing certain current events, but courts are more likely to weigh up the actual benefits (as they see them) that may arise from reporting those events. The media's contribution towards those events would then be assessed.

The Press Complaints Commission (PCC) Editors' Code of Practice incorporates a specific definition of the public interest:

> The public interest includes, but is not confined to: i) Detecting or exposing crime or serious impropriety. ii) Protecting public health and

safety. iii) Preventing the public from being misled by an action or statement of an individual or organization.

(PCC, 2011)

The PCC offers the further advice to editors that it requires them to fully demonstrate that they 'reasonably believed that publication, or journalistic activity undertaken with a view to publication, would be in the public interest and how, and with whom, that was established at the time' (PCC, 2011). It should be noted that the industry self-regulatory body was dissolved by its own board in March 2012, and a transitional body was earmarked to replace it, in the wake of the phone-hacking scandal and subsequent Leveson Inquiry (O'Carroll, 2012).

Morrison *et al.* (2007, pp. 354–7) have undertaken extensive focus-group and nationally representative surveys into people's responses as to what constitutes the public interest. People's responses were sought to a set of storylines (e.g. 'Foods sold by a major supermarket have been contaminated by bacteria', or, 'a member of a leading pop group has cosmetic surgery to change her face shape'). Morrison and his colleagues found that some media coverage was clearly 'majority public interest' (the first example) and thus more universally considered so, while other coverage was clearly 'minority public interest' (the second example), and tended towards constituting more personal interest. Their conclusion was that 'for many people, public interest is understood to mean something beyond purely personal interest', and that the majority of people did not view 'gossip' media stories as being of public interest (ibid., p. 356).

There was clear evidence that people discriminate strongly between the extent to which different kinds of broadly 'public-interest' stories were covered by the media. So, for example, the individuals surveyed thought that certain kinds of topics warranted their level of coverage (crime and local/community stories), and these stories had the potential to have an impact at an individual and a societal level. On the other hand, coverage of local politicians' public lives was seen by 88 per cent of those surveyed to be warranted – but only 40 per cent thought their private lives worthy of coverage. However these public/private distinctions did not extend to the media coverage of sports personalities or rock stars (p. 357). Morrison *et al.*'s research indicated an expectation of the watchdog function in line with democratic ideals of the media as a Fourth Estate. Interestingly, unlike some other research about responses to concerns in media coverage over matters of taste and decency, this research indicates a fairly consistent set of demographic responses to meanings of the public interest and the media.

The survey also asked respondents for definitions of 'the public interest' in their own words, which generated a number of broader categorizations and subcategories:

- *Public-service ethos (65 per cent):* public rights (34 per cent); public effects (28 per cent); and national interest (3 per cent).
- *Consumer-oriented (24 per cent):* interests of the public (15 per cent); personal interests (7 per cent); and local/community interest (2 per cent).
- *Media practice-based (33 per cent):* unwarranted intrusion (16 per cent); media excuse (12 per cent); and warranted intrusion (5 per cent).

These ideas about the public interest range from information-seeking, rights-based notions, or satisfying other 'needs' (consumer entertainments) through to various kinds of media actions that are unwarranted or justified, or just accepted as intrinsic to the media's role (Morrison *et al.*, 2007, pp. 358–62).

Echoing the Morrison *et al.* practice-based definitions, it has been argued that ideas of *serving* the public interest are often connected with an argument that media companies are not ordinary businesses. The argument is that, if the media are successfully performing their role in a democratic polity, then they will be providing critical information to citizens (McQuail, 1992, p. 70; Shultz, 1994). In this way media performance, as Maras notes, is rightly focused on holding the media accountable in their public-interest role (Maras, 2007).

Clearly there are specific matters in the public interest, involving a direct information provision for accountability purposes that deserve media scrutiny. They would include issues relating to the performance of institutions of government, their elected representatives and civil servants, corporations and their executives and other civil-society organizations.

Importantly, the notion of public interest can often be closely linked to revelation or disclosure. The high-profile scandals that occur beyond the public gaze are grist to the mill in this category, and are a constant feature of the media in all countries, and usually the motivation to report them will be a mix of profit and fourth-estate ideals (Tiffen, 1999).

The Public Interest in Media Regulation

Peter Lunt and Sonia Livingstone have explored how the new breed of 'convergent' media regulators, such as Ofcom or ACMA, might ensure that updated ideas of the public interest are repositioned at the heart of regulatory processes (2007, p. 2). In their view a regulatory struggle is yet to resolve the balance of consumer and industry, and consumer and citizen interests, in the reformulation of the public interest. They see a primary tension in this regard between, on the one hand, the need to regulate a market so that it is 'competitive and delivers good value to consumers', and on the other, 'the need to protect citizens from risk and detriment' (ibid.).

When the term 'citizen' appeared during the debates of the Communications Act, 2003 it emerged very much as a contested term. Under the Act Ofcom is legally obliged to consider citizens' interests. For example, Ofcom's Content Board is charged with 'understanding, analysing and championing' the voices of the 'viewers, listeners and citizens' (Ofcom, 2011). Ofcom explains the function of its Content Board as specifically seeing that: 'its public interest agenda is prioritized ... by examining issues where the citizen interest extends beyond the consumer interest ... with a focus on those aspects of the public interest which competition and market forces do not reach' (ibid.).

Feintuck, in his analysis of the establishment of Ofcom, takes the view that, despite the recommendations of the Puttnam Committee, which scrutinized the Draft Communications Bill 2002, that Ofcom embodies 'the long term interests of all citizens', public interests are not necessarily well represented in the practical realities of modern media regulation (Feintuck, 2004, p. 94; Feintuck and Varney, 2006, pp. 114–25). When the Communications Act 2003 came into force, his observation is that the 'vulnerability of broad public interests in media regulation has not been satisfactorily remedied by the Communications Act 2003' (ibid., p. 115).

In his opinion the contemporary UK regulatory focus can be characterized in this way:

In the context of ongoing trends of technological development and convergence, and corporate conglomeration in the media industries, the previously dominant 'public service' tradition in British broadcasting has been replaced by a model in which regulators must justify their interventions in relation primarily to the economics of the market. From a citizen-oriented vision embodied in the public service tradition, regulation has turned its focus to an agenda derived from perceptions of consumer interests, contributing to and reconfirming the commodification of the media within an increasingly producer-led, free-market media economy.

(Feintuck, 2004, pp. 94–5)

His argument is that these conditions, which are by no means unique to the media industries, have developed historically from the deregulatory *Zeitgeist* of the Thatcher/Regan era, downplaying the key role of the media and replacing it with a consumerist market-driven framework. For Feintuck, then, 'the democratic significance of the media is unquestioned, and permits substantial public interest claims, in terms of collective values which ... go far beyond the consumerist expectations of choice'.

In their analysis Lunt and Livingstone describe other ongoing tensions between the needs of individual consumers and broader public policy objectives, and consumer protections and consumer awareness-raising policies. They note that regulation in the public interest is bundled with discourses of more media-literate consumers, where regulators act with a 'light touch', guided by claims to 'evidence-based' rationales (Lunt and Livingstone, 2007, p. 2).

The ACMA interprets the maintenance of the public interest in regulation in terms of the need to balance citizen and consumer interests. In *'Citizens' and the ACMA – Exploring the Concepts within Australian Media and Communications Regulation*, the regulator suggests that in the context of the delivery and regulation of media and communications its brand of 'citizen filter' can be activated in terms of service delivery, encouraging active citizen contribution; regulating in the public interest; and educating, informing and advising citizens. Perhaps more significantly though, the paper suggests that 'citizen interests' provide 'a means of amplifying the regulator's public interest objectives' (ACMA, 2010, p. 9).

Lesley Hitchens has written extensively on the importance of terminology used in media policy debates (Hitchens, 2007). In a submission to an Australian government inquiry into convergence she makes the point:

> How 'the public' and 'the public interest' is characterized can have an important influence on the shaping of media policy. Recognizing that the public can have different identities, for example, 'the public as citizen' or 'the public as consumer' can contribute to a better understanding of what interests may be at stake in different communications scenarios. In turn, this understanding can contribute to the design of policy and regulatory settings.
>
> (Hitchens, 2011)

Hitchens is not suggesting a preference for consumer or citizen constructions of the public interest, but rather that both may exist together for a particular topic. Her key argument is that in any discussions of 'the public interest' or the public more generally, it's important that policy makers explain precisely which meanings they intend to convey.

News Content in Democracies

Governments and their regulatory agencies recognize an ongoing public interest in maintaining a pluralistic news media, and thus a sufficient number of independent news voices, in order to sustain a healthy democracy (Fenton, 2010)). But mergers and acquisitions in the media sector frequently test the operation of media-ownership and control laws. I've argued elsewhere that constant pressure from opposing (private) interests is brought to bear against these laws (Dwyer, 2010).

A proposal by News Corporation in 2010–11 to take full ownership (from 39 per cent to 61 per cent) of British Sky Broadcasting (BSkyB) was an event that concentrated the minds of the Cameron government and its regulatory agencies. The possibility that News Corporation could own a swathe of the newspaper sector (currently approximately 37 per cent), three of the top ten most trafficked news websites with its News International assets, as well as a dominant position in the highly popular satellite broadcaster – in particular as Sky News channel has around 35 per cent of the TV market (*Financial Times*, 2011), quite rightly, set off alarms. The political and regulatory response to this deal was a litmus test for media-ownership laws, and the policy implications of twenty-first-century cross-media ownership throughout the world.

Jeremy Hunt, the UK's then culture secretary, under his role specified in the Enterprise Act 2002, investigated News Corporation's proposed acquisition of BSkyB. Hunt was required to decide whether he should refer the £8.3 billion merger to the EU Competition Commission to see whether the deal would have an adverse impact on news markets (with Ofcom having already formed this view). Opponents of the deal argued that the corporation's influence on the UK media landscape would simply be too great if it had full control of BSkyB and its £950 million cash flow. Initially Hunt chose not to refer the merger to the Competition Commission as recommended by Ofcom and, in spite of this, he publicly released the Ofcom report. His intentions were apparently to allow the deal to proceed without even being considered by the Competition Commission, as required by the public interest (or 'plurality test') process for mergers (*Financial Times*, 2011).

Questions were raised regarding whether his actions were in the public interest; Hunt decided to begin direct negotiations with News

Corporation(Watson and Hickman, 2012, pp. 144–146). The Secretary of State's European intervention notice for the public interest is concerned with the plurality of control of media enterprises, that is:

> the need, in relation to every different audience in the United Kingdom or in a particular area or locality of the United Kingdom, for there to be a sufficient plurality of persons with control of the media enterprises serving that audience.
>
> (Enterprise Act 2002, s.58(2c)(a))

Ofcom's concerns centred on news provision. Inevitably, the potential cross-media combination of News Corporation's and BSkyB's news assets – the News International newspapers and Sky News – was the focus of the regulator's attention. Ofcom's 'invitation to comment' document revealed the main factors it was required to consider in weighing up whether the deal would adversely affect the public interest. In essence, Ofcom's core interest was focusing on the 'need for sufficient media plurality in the functioning of a healthy and informed democratic society'.

To this end, Ofcom sought comment on the likely impact of the acquisition on:

- content types;
- audiences;
- media platforms;
- control of media enterprises;
- future developments in the media landscape.

> (Ofcom, 2010)

Under the 'media platforms' category, Ofcom was specifically interested in the internet platform when reviewing the implications of the proposed acquisition. The regulator noted that it would: 'consider how future market developments, including the convergence of broadcast, print and internet media may affect consumers' consumption of relevant media and the current levels of media plurality'. In broad terms, the purpose of the Ofcom plurality test is to assess: 'how the proposed acquisition may affect the level of plurality of persons with control of the media enterprises serving the relevant audiences' (ibid., 1.10 and 1.12).

As noted earlier, in early March 2011 Hunt approved News Corporation's takeover of BSkyB, despite being 'very aware' of criticisms of the threat to media plurality, and people's 'suspicions of the motives of politicians' (Press Association, 2011). The deal would not be referred to the Competition Commission in Brussels, which had been Ofcom's preference. The main features of the takeover in the deal negotiated by News Corporation were:

- the board of Sky News would have a non-executive, independent chairman and a majority of non-executive, independent directors;
- News proposed that shares in Sky News be distributed among existing shareholders, with Mr Murdoch's company maintaining its 39 per cent holding;
- News would not be allowed to increase its shareholding without the permission of the culture secretary for ten years;
- News would provide funding in the form of 'a substantial revenue stream' to Sky News for ten years.

Media academic Steven Barnett assessed the public-interest risk:

> This deal raises profound questions over what will happen to the ownership of Sky News in the longer term – who will make senior editorial appointments and for how long a so-called separation of one channel from a corporate parent can be sustained

Other commentators feared it would irreversibly change the UK news media landscape for the worse, creating the largest news organization in the country (BBC, 2011).

In the event the fate of the deal was determined, at least in the short term, by the rapidly changing fortunes of News Corporation following its decision to close the 168-year-old *News of the World*, and the sustained public furore arising from the phone-hacking scandal. On 14 July News Corporation's thirteen-month campaign to fully own BSkyB was terminated. In order to pre-empt a reversal of the decision that was almost in the bag, and in an effort to stem a haemorrhaging share price, News had made a calculated decision to withdraw its bid. Some commentators speculated that the bid may be reignited at a later date, after hostile public opinion has subsided (Shoebridge, 2011). After phone-hacking and Leveson, such an outcome now seems remote.

The Ethics of Media Reform

The moral challenge for governments in regulating new media in the public interest is to develop a plurality test capable of taking into account convergence *and* concentration across all platforms, including the internet. Behind this challenge are a rapidly changing media industry and the business models which have previously sustained that industry: at their heart is the increase in online advertising, which has an annual international growth rate of around 10 per cent (Ofcom, 2009).

All the evidence suggests that changing industry-revenue structures will need to be taken into account in any policy and regulatory responses by the government to ownership and convergence.

The new 'attention economy' has important consequences for key 'democracy-maintaining' genres such as news. A number of studies have shown that the sources of news in online and mobile media contexts are funnelled through a small number of dominant news brands and media organizations, search engines and portals.

For example, US scholar Matthew Hindman has found:

A substantial majority of searches contain the names of specific news outlets or specific Web pages. Of the 990 total searches, 595 – three-fifths – were searches for specific Web sites or online news outlets. In short, most searches involve citizens seeking out news organizations they are already familiar with.

(2009, p. 73)

The authors of a recent OECD report have expressed their concern that existing laws to promote diversity of ownership (and therefore viewpoints) are inadequate in the face of multiplatform distribution of news (2010, p. 78).

The reality of 'where and how consumers get their news' is an important issue for all democracies in relation to any reassessment of existing media-diversity/pluralism policy objectives. This discussion offers further support for the idea that the cross-platform usage of news media needs to continue to inform policy development.

In light of these industry and audience user trends, a critical ethical issue is how governments and their regulatory agencies adapt existing media laws, and construct new normative policy principles to promote diversity of control (and therefore viewpoints) for influential mass-consumption media. In particular, in the area of critical information genres such as news, there is a strong reformist argument that governments should develop a plurality test capable of taking into account convergence *and* concentration across all platforms, including the internet, however accessed.

Although there is considerable uncertainty regarding the precise rate of change in the transition of mass audiences to online and mobile media, many agree that the role of government and regulators must be to maintain core social and political principles in the public interest. The responsibility of governments when it comes to convergent media is a profoundly moral one in shaping media environments: this is a question of maintaining public access to affordable, diverse and high-quality content. The content that really matters in a democracy is richly informational, news and current-affairs content.

References

ACMA (2010) *'Citizens' and the ACMA – Exploring the Concepts within Australian Media and Communications Regulation*, Occasional Paper, June, Australian Media and Communications Authority.
APC (2009) *Statement of Principles*, available at http://www.presscouncil.org.au/pcsite/complaints/sop.html.
Baker, C. E. (2007) *Media Concentration and Democracy: Why Ownership Matters* (New York: Cambridge University Press).
Barnouw, E. (1956) *Mass Communication: Television, Radio, Film, Press: The Media and Their Practice in the United States of America* (New York: Holt, Rinehart and Winston).
BBC (2011) 'Rupert Murdoch BSkyB Takeover Gets Government Go-ahead', 3 March, available at http://www.bbc.co.uk/news/business-12631875.
DBCDE (2011) *Convergence Framing Paper*, June, Department of Broadband Communications and the Digital Economy.
DBCDE (2012) Convergence Review, Final Report, March, *Department of Broad Band Communications and the Digital Economy*.
Dennis, E. E. and J. C. Merrill (2005) *Media Debates: Great Issues for the Digital Age* (Belmont, CA: Thomson Wadsworth).
Dwyer, T. (2010) *Media Convergence* (Maidenhead: McGraw-Hill, Open University Press).
Dwyer, T. with F. Martin and G. Goggin (2011) *Submission to the Department of Broadband Communications and the Digital Economy's Convergence Review*, January.
European Commission (2007) Press Release, 'Media Pluralism: Commission Stresses Need for Transparency, Freedom and Diversity in Europe's Media Landscape', Press Release, Brussels, 16 January, available at http://www.europa.eu/rapid/pressReleasesAction.do?reference=IP/07/52&format=HTML&aged=0&language=EN&guiLanguage=fr.
Feintuck, M. (2004) *The Public Interest in Regulation* (Oxford: Oxford University Press).
Feintuck, M. and M. Varney (2006) *Media Regulation, Public Interest and the Law*, 2nd edn (Edinburgh: Edinburgh University Press).
Fenton, N. (ed). (2010) *New Media, Old News, Journalism and Democracy in a Digital Age* (London: Sage).
Financial Times (2011) Editorial, 'Call off the Hunt', *FT.com.uk*, 20 January.
Hindman, M. (2009) *The Myth of Digital Democracy* (Princeton, NJ: Princeton University Press).

Hitchens, L. (2007) 'Citizen versus Consumer in the Digital World', in A. T. Kenyon (ed.), *TV Futures: Digital Television Policy in Australia*, pp. 343–63.

Hitchens, L. (2011) *Submission to DBCDE Convergence Review*. Department of Broadband Communications and the Digital Economy, available at http://www.dbcde.gov.au/submissions/20110124_15.24.30/27-Lesley%20 Hitchens.pdf.

Hitwise (2007) *News and Media Report*, April, available at www.hitwise.com.

Keane, J. (2010) *The Life and Death of Democracy* (London: Pocket Books/Simon and Schuster).

Lunt, P. and S. Livingstone (2007) 'Regulation in the Public Interest', *Consumer Policy Review* vol. 17 no. 2.

Maras, S. (2007) 'Media Law and Ethics', Lecture 12 Notes, University of Sydney.

McQuail, Denis (1992) 'The Public Interest in Communication', in *Media Performance: Mass Communication and the Public Interest* (London: Sage).

MEAA (2010) *Life in the Clickstream: The Future of Journalism*, Media Entertainment and Arts Alliance, Sydney, December, p. 36, available at http://www.thefuture-ofjournalism.org.au/.

Morrison, D., M. Kieran, M. Svennevig and S. Ventress (2007) *Media and Values: Intimate Transgressions in a Changing Moral and Cultural Landscape* (Bristol and Chicago, IL Intellect).

O'Carroll, L. (2012) 'Press Complaints Commission to Close in Wake of Phone-hacking Scandal', *Guardian*, 8 March, available at http://www.guardian. co.uk/media/2012/mar/08/press-complaints-commission-close-phone-hacking.

OECD (2010) DSTI/ICCP/IE(2009)14/FINAL, *The Evolution of News and the Internet*, Working Party on the Information Economy, 11 June, p. 78.

Ofcom (2009) *The International Communications Market Report*, available at http://stakeholders.ofcom.org.uk/market-data-research/market-data/ communications-market-reports/icmr09/.

Ofcom (2010) 'Invitation to Comment for Public Interest Test on the Anticipated Acquisition of British Sky Broadcasting plc by News Corporation', 5 November.

Ofcom (2011) 'Content Board Functions and Role', available at http://www. ofcom.org.uk/about/how-ofcom-is-run/content-board/functions-and-role/.

Press Association (2011) 'Murdoch BSkyB Takeover Moves Closer', 3 March, available at http://www.pressassociation.com/component/pafeeds/2011/03/03/ murdoch_bskyb_takeover_moves_closer?camefrom=news.

Press Complaints Commission (2011) Editors' Code of Practice, available at http://www.pcc.org.uk/cop/practice.html.

Shultz, J. (1994) *Not Just Another Business: Journalists, Citizens and the Media*, Melbourne: Pluto Press.

Shoebridge, N. (2011) 'New BSkyB Bid at Least Two Years Away', *Australian Financial Review*, 15 July.

Sorauf, F. J. (1957) 'The Public Interest Reconsidered', *Journal of Politics* vol. 19 no. 4, pp. 616–39.

Spence, E. H., A. Alexandra, A. Quinn and A. Dunn (2011) *Media, Markets, and Morals* (Malden, MA and Oxford: Wiley-Blackwell).

Tiffen, R. (1999) *Scandals: Media, Politics and Corruption in Contemporary Australia*, Sydney: UNSW Press.

Watson, T. and Hickman, M. (2012) *Dial M for Murdoch, News Corporation and the Corruption of Britain* (London: Allen lane/Penguin).

7 Conclusion

Legal and Ethical Issues in the Media has introduced readers to the importance of media practitioners possessing a toolkit of legal, ethical and media-practice skills and knowledges, in order to produce quality content for an informed citizenry. Earlier chapters discussed the issues, legal concepts and ethical frameworks for reflecting on media practice. We also explored legal and ethical literacies by considering some of the basic constituent elements of interacting legal, ethical and media systems.

Media practitioners are subject to the same laws as are all other citizens. Yet everyone who publishes on any media platform needs to be mindful of the potential to defame or breach contempt laws, to breach a confidence, to illegally invade privacy or to breach copyright. However, safe publishing does not require a lawyer's knowledge, but rather an awareness of the boundaries of particular laws. Breaches of media law are constantly occurring but, equipped with a working knowledge of concepts, frameworks and general legal literacies relevant to their roles as content creators, as we have discussed throughout this book, media practitioners will be able to confidently and effectively work in the evolving media and communications industries.

Media practices will also always benefit from analysis based on best-practice professional and ethical judgment, informed by the long history of ethical philosophy. In this concluding chapter we will briefly review enduring priorities for media practitioners, who find themselves in the midst of ongoing transformations in the media and communications industries. But first let me recap some important points.

In looking at the way that defamation law seeks to maintain a healthy balance between free communication and the protection of reputations, we've seen how defamation frameworks vary across Anglophone common-law jurisdictions and cultures. In this sense, defamation laws also represent a moral discourse inscribed with political priorities concerning media speech and reputations.

Similarly, our evolving notions of privacy can be seen as a struggle between public interests desiring an unfettered means of communication against a backdrop of another set of public interests: calls for enhanced privacy safeguards for individuals. The increasing use of new media and communications technologies is now inevitably implicated in this evolution. Fine-tuning the law in this area is a complex and politicized process: it's important to protect individual privacy, but equally, the media must be allowed to report matters of legitimate public concern.

As the Hargreaves report *Digital Opportunity: A Review of Intellectual Property and Growth* (2011) argues, the realignment of technological capacities and media-consumption practices has led to a questioning of the sustainability of mainstream intellectual-property business models. A key finding was that laws designed more than three centuries ago, with the express purpose of creating economic incentives for innovation by protecting creators' rights, are today obstructing innovation and economic growth by both rights holders and consumers.

The discussion in Chapter 6 was centrally concerned with large-scale corporate media consolidation, as a live application of the term 'public interest'. The argument was made that key ethical questions arise from the fundamental structuring of media systems in market societies. Media plurality, ownership policies, accountability and responsibility in media and politics need to be seen as interconnected. Ethical questions regarding the standards of journalism flow from these corporate cultures within news-media organizations.

In this regard it's worth concluding the book with a short overview of the UK's phone-hacking scandal to date, referred to earlier in the book, to look at how it escalated and then broadened out to engulf many more people than it was initially thought to involve. At the time of writing, judicial, parliamentary and police inquiries continued into these unprecedented events. The pervasive extent of corrupt practices surprised even the most savvy media practitioners. But the events are perhaps a little less shocking if we remember that the phone-hacking scandal occurred at a time of general decline in both the readership and revenue of the traditional bricks-and-mortar newspaper industry. So they serve as indicators of the risks taken by media practitioners, and the depths to which commercial media operations are prepared to sink, in order to remain profitable.

It began with one title, the *News of the World*, a royal family correspondent, Clive Goodman and a private investigator, Glenn Mulcaire, both jailed in 2007 for phone-hacking offences. At a subsequent parliamentary inquiry News International flatly denied that others were involved in these activities. Relentless reporting by the *Guardian*, and then a police investigation, revealed that these illegal activities went much further (Fenton, 2011).

The scandal initially led to the resignation of Andy Coulson, first in 2007 from his position as editor of the *News of the World*, then, in 2011, from his role as prime minister David Cameron's press secretary, and to the arrests of three senior *News of the World* journalists by the Metropolitan Police. The early police investigations found hundreds of names, of celebrities, politicians, PR agents and also a number of PIN numbers for cell phones in Mulcaire's home. It was therefore very plausible that this was an endemic practice within parts of the culture of the print media industry. Subsequently, in 2011, it came to light that hundreds of individuals' phones were hacked, including the phone of thirteen-year-old murdered schoolgirl, Milly Dowler, and those of families of soldiers who had served in Iraq. Other consequences included an additional six reporters and editors being arrested, including the former editor of the *News of the World*, followed by News International chief executive Rebekah Brooks, and senior police resignations, including that of Metropolitan Police Commissioner Sir Paul Stephenson. Pressure was on David Cameron to resign as prime minister.

As the British establishment reeled from the unravelling links of corrupt practices and their related arrests and resignations in politics, the media and police ranks, the message in large flashing neon lights was that abuse of media power, commercial greed and public deception had been tolerated for too long.

It was confirmed by the Murdochs in their extraordinary appearance before the parliamentary home affairs committee in July 2011 that Mulcaire's legal costs were still being paid for by News International. *Guardian* columnist, and now academic, Roy Greenslade, quite rightly, questioned the moral integrity of such an arrangement where a man has been 'convicted of intercepting voicemail messages (and) he has served months in jail' (ABC, 2011).

When News Corporation strategically shelved its BSkyB deal to get 100 per cent control, coupled with the uncertainty about the future of News Corporation and the Murdoch dynasty, the share price fell. The gravity of wrongdoing was also evident in the decision by the US Federal Bureau of Investigation to commence an investigation into whether the victims of 9/11 in New York or their family members' phones had been hacked; a Department of Justice investigation was also begun into whether alleged payments to UK police may have contravened the Foreign Corrupt Practices Act (Rappeport, 2011). But perhaps of most consequence of all in the fall-out from the phone-hacking scandal was the further undermining of public trust in the professional culture of journalism itself.

However, on top of the opprobrium directed at the wrongdoers, other murkier issues concerning professional conduct and risk were highlighted by this particular media scandal. The breach of relevant communication-interception laws was relatively straightforward. On the other hand, the ethics of news gathering is more problematic: as we've seen, codes of practice provide general guidance about honesty, fairness, accuracy and integrity, but their ability to stem, and then apply meaningful sanctions to more systemic patterns of conduct arising from the general ethos of an industry context, is doubtful. This is where the valorized priorities of media practitioners, and the cultures of particular media organizations engendering them, become very significant (Dennis and Merrill, 2006, p. 130). Indeed, according to one recently retired Australian politician with a reputation for integrity, it's closely bound up with the whole media 'sideshow' syndrome (Tanner, 2011).

An interesting side story to emerge from the phone-hacking scandal has been the manner in which News International co-opted the legal system, in effect as part of a media-relations strategy. Foreseeing that high-profile witnesses in open court would result in ongoing damaging media coverage, News chose another approach: a so-called 'voluntary compensation scheme' for victims of phone hacking. (This was separate to hundreds of thousands of pounds in payments to high-profile victims such as PR guru Max Clifford, characterized by some as 'hush money'.) Its offer, for those who agreed to settle outside court, was that they receive a 10 per cent bonus in a compensation award 'on top of the amount a High Court judge might award' (Fenton, 2011). Sir Charles Gray, a High Court judge, agreed to act as an adjudicator in the award of damages. News regognized the benefits of the scheme, including a more expeditious process than the court could offer, confidentiality and no risk of legal costs.

The economic power of big media corporations allows them to clear regulatory hurdles, and in some cases, control their own moral fates. This can be seen in the role, for example, that Google Corporation plays when it is able to buy its way out of ethico-legal hot water. In a quarterly statement filed with the US Securities and Exchange Commission the diversified new media behemoth revealed that it had set aside $US500 million as a war-chest to settle a legal and regulatory investigation into aspects of its search-advertising business. This admission was made in the wake of separate battles with the US Department of Justice and the Federal Trade Commission regarding abuse of market power and antitrust issues (Waters and Menn, 2011).

Enduring Legal and Ethical Concerns

The ways in which media are produced, distributed and consumed by audiences continue to change relatively rapidly. Communications media are constantly undergoing significant transformations – in this era of deregulation, concentrating ownership and the internet. Therefore it is important to recognize that the fundamental debates involving communication and society both change and stay the same. An important implication of this evolutionary process is that the traditional media of television, radio and newspapers are changing alongside the popular new media forms. Accordingly, many of the laws that have been developed in the context of existing media are also relevant to new media, such as the internet and social-media applications.

The architecture of our media is itself a critical moral issue for our times, in a similar way to the problem of climate change. The laws and policies drafted by elected officials have long-term consequences for the way people lead their lives. As we saw in Chapter 6, governments are ultimately responsible in an age of converging media for shaping our digital media environments: at its heart this is a question of maintaining public access to affordable, diverse and high-quality content. The enduring concerns for society include a wider set of legal, policy and regulatory questions that grapple with matters of moral consequence for audiences such as: the media and democracy; media concentration and ownership; universal service and net neutrality; the representation of race, ethnicity and other diversities; responsibility for young audiences; and the provision of services for less able audiences (Dwyer, 2010).

Behind many of these enduring concerns we can identify a further set of concepts that privilege bigger-picture, systemic ideas, which focus on the well-being of citizens and consumers and a commitment to 'good regulatory design' (Chapman, 2011).

Clearly, traditional concerns do not just disappear merely because of new media production, distribution and consumption methods: rather, new legal and ethical issues are constantly emerging. Changing social and cultural uses arise through innovation in media and communication practices, including developments in the way people are using media while in transit and drawing on location-based applications (and accessing content that can originate from almost anywhere in the world), and with the ease of falsifying identity and information in general. As social and cultural uses of media evolve, these will find expression in the law. The law, after all, is a formal system for the governance of culture.

References

ABC (2011) ABC Television, Lateline programme. 'Former Editor Calls for UK Phone Scandal Inquiry', 21 April, available at http://www.abc.net.au/lateline/content/2011/s3198527.htm.

Chapman, C. (2011) 'The "Convergence Phenomena" from a Regulator's Perspective', Speech to the Communications and Media Law Association, 30 May, available at www.acma.gov.au.

Dennis, E. E. and J. C. Merrill (2006) *Media Debates: Great Issues for the Digital Age*, 4th edn (Belmont, CA: Thomson Wadsworth).

Dwyer, T. (2010) *Media Convergence* (Maidenhead: McGraw-Hill/Open University Press).

Fenton, B. (2011) 'Newspaper Offers Deal to Phone Hack Victims', *Financial Times.com*, 16 June, available at http://www.ft.com/intl/cms/s/0/d7378fd4-9844-11e0-ae45-00144feab49a.html?ftcamp=rss&ftcamp=crm/email/2011617/nbe/MediaInternet/product#axzz1Pm92o46J.

Hargreaves, I. (2001) *Digital Opportunity: A Review of Intellectual Property and Growth*, Intellectual Property Office, May, available at http://www.ipo.gov.uk/ipreview-finalreport.pdf.

Rappeport, A. (2011) 'Hacking Case Linked to US News Corp Arm Referred to FBI', *Financial Times.com*, 20 July, available at http://www.ft.com/intl/cms/s/0/fbe021de-b2f2-11e0-86b8-00144feabdc0.html#axzz1Sis2rNg7.

Tanner, L. (2011) *Sideshow: Dumbing Down Democracy* (Melbourne: Scribe).

Waters, R. and J. Menn (2011) 'Google Sets Aside $500 Million for US Probe', *Financial Times.com*, 11 May, available at http://www.ft.com/cms/s/0/2edb7b9c-7b5d-11e0-ae56-00144feabdc0.html?ftcamp=rss#axzz1Pm92o46J.

Index